THE FRUIT-PICKING GUIDE
AUSTRALIA

Find a job, calendar of seasons and farm contacts and addresses

EDITION 2020

HELPSTAGE
Internship offers

WWW.HELPSTAGE.COM

HELPSTAGE
Internship offers

Code ISBN :9781655588099

SUMMARY

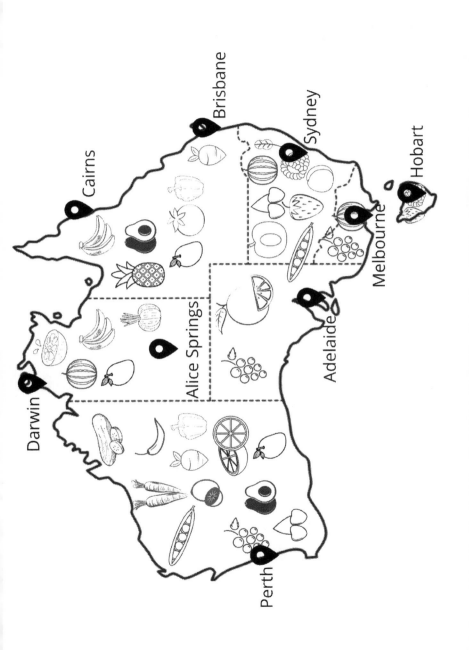

THE PREREQUISITES

The visa application
To be able to work on a farm in Australia, you must get a Working Holiday Visa. To do this, you must be between 18 and 35 years old (30 years old depending on your country), have AU$5,000 in your bank account and be in possession of a passport from one of the following countries:
Belgium, France, Luxembourg, Canada, Cyprus, Denmark, Estonia, Finland, Germany, Hong Kong, Ireland, Italy, Japan, Korea, Malta, Netherlands, Norway, Sweden, Taiwan, United Kingdom, Argentina, Bangladesh, Chile, Indonesia, Malaysia, Thailand, Turkey, United States and Uruguay.
The 13 countries under negotiation with Australia: Andorra, Brazil, Croatia, Fiji, India, Latvia, Lithuania, Mexico, Monaco, Mongolia, Philippines, Solomon Islands and Switzerland.

Why do I need AU$5,000 in the bank account?
Australian immigration wants to ensure that all workers arriving in Australia have sufficient financial resources to be able to support themselves for the first few weeks.

The process

THE VISA APPLICATION

Open the page:

https://immi.homeaffairs.gov.au/visas/getting-a-visa/visa-listing/work-holiday-417

Working Holiday visa (subclass 417)

Features

This visa is for young people who want to holiday and work in Australia for up to a year.

Requirements

You might be able to get this visa if you:

- are at least 18 but not yet 31 years of age
- do not have a dependent child accompanying you at any time during your stay in Australia
- have a passport from an eligible country.

You might be able to apply online by clicking the 'Apply now' button below, if you have a passport from an eligible country. See 'How to Apply' for a list of eligible countries.

If you cannot apply online you can lodge a paper application form.

⇨ **Apply Now**

Download PDF Form

A window opens. Click on "create an ImmiAccount"

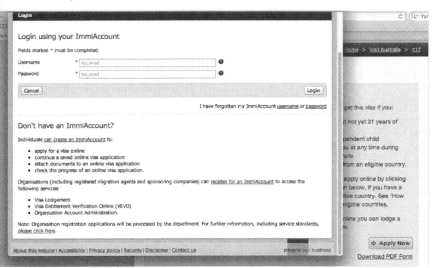

4

Fill in all the required information in the fields.

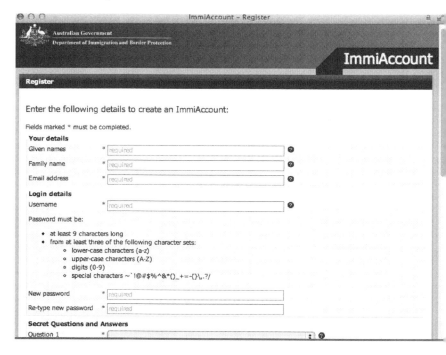

Once you have completed the online form, you will receive a confirmation email. Then simply click on the link received to confirm your email.

A new window will open. Click on 'I have read and agree to the terms and conditions'.

How long will my visa be valid?
The visa allows you to work for one year in Australia, including 6 consecutive months for the same employer.

Click on "next".

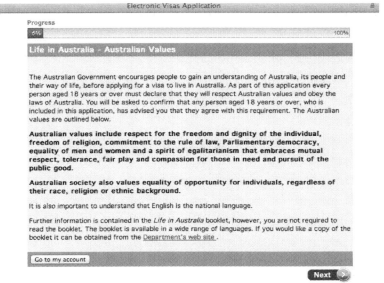

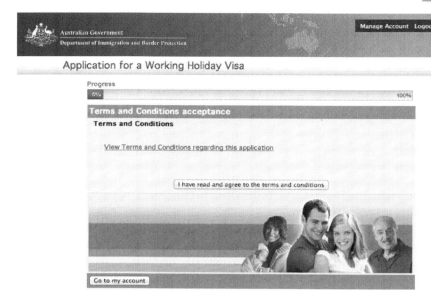

Fill in your details and click on "Next" at the bottom.

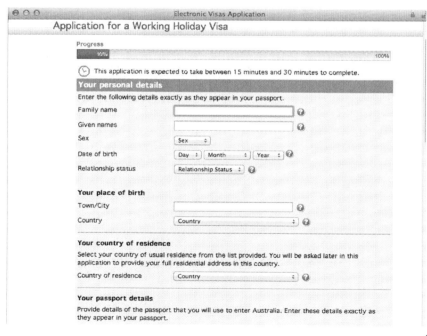

Answer the 3 questions about your status and what you plan to do when you arrive in Australia.

(You can follow the progress of your request at the top of the page in green).

Click on "Next" when you have answered the questions.

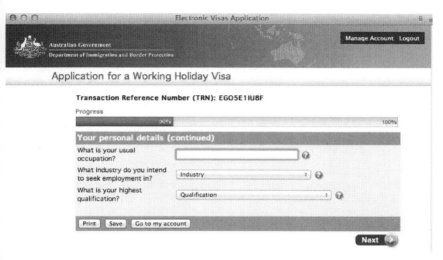

A transaction number appears in a new window. You must then fill in all the fields and click on "Next".

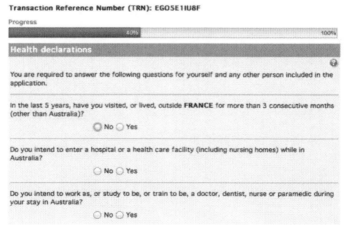

Ditto. Answer NO to the following questions.

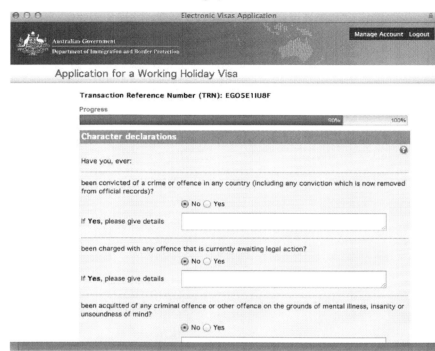

You are now at 95% of the process. These are just questions to verify what you just said.
Answer all questions.

How much is the visa?
The visa costs 485 AU$.

Can I leave Australia and come back during this year?
Yes, you can go out as many times as you like until your Working Holida Visa expires.

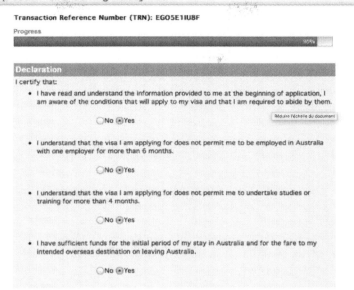

Application for a Working Holiday Visa

Transaction Reference Number (TRN): EGO5E1IU8F

Progress

95%

Declaration

I certify that:

- I have read and understand the information provided to me at the beginning of application, I am aware of the conditions that will apply to my visa and that I am required to abide by them.

  ◯ No ⦿ Yes

  Réduire l'échelle du document

- I understand that the visa I am applying for does not permit me to be employed in Australia with one employer for more than 6 months.

  ◯ No ⦿ Yes

- I understand that the visa I am applying for does not permit me to undertake studies or training for more than 4 months.

  ◯ No ⦿ Yes

- I have sufficient funds for the initial period of my stay in Australia and for the fare to my intended overseas destination on leaving Australia.

  ◯ No ⦿ Yes

On the next page, check all the information about yourself. A new window opens. Click on "Submit now".

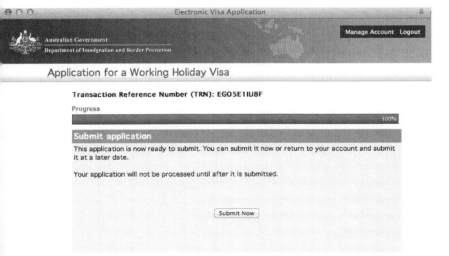

Electronic Visa Application

Manage Account   Logout

Australian Government
Department of Immigration and Border Protection

Application for a Working Holiday Visa

Transaction Reference Number (TRN): EGO5E1IU8F

Progress

100%

Submit application

This application is now ready to submit. You can submit it now or return to your account and submit it at a later date.

Your application will not be processed until after it is submitted.

[Submit Now]

10

You now arrive on the AU$485 payment page, and once it is done, all you have to do is wait to receive an email saying:'**Visa granted**'.
It takes between a few hours and a month.
You can choose to make the payment later and return to your account whenever you wish and click on the'Manage Payment' link.

You will need to download two additional documents: the passport and the bank statement proving AU$5,000 into your account. It may happen that when you upload the documents to the site, it does not work. You must then change the name of your documents and try again. If this still doesn't work, it's because there's a bug on the site.
This often happens so don't worry. Just come back to your account later to try again.

How long will it take to receive my visa?

13 days for 70% of requests.
22 days for 90% of requests.
Some candidates receive their visas only a few hours after making their payment. If this may come as a surprise, yes it is your visa as long as it is well written in the email "**Visa Granted**".

The visa is a number received by email. Your visa will be validated at the Australian Immigration and will be valid for one year.
You can leave the country as many times as you wish during the 12 months of your visa.

Apply for your second visa: 88 days in a farm to stay 2 years in Australia

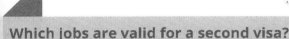

Which jobs are valid for a second visa?

Cultivation of plants/animal breeding.
Fishing and pearl culture
Arboriculture and felling
Mining operations
Construction

Woofing (unpaid work) also works if it
falls into the categories mentioned above.

To get a second **Working Holiday Visa**, and therefore be able to stay in Australia for 2 years, you will have to work 88 days in a farm, twice as long if you want to stay for 3 years.

This is what many backpackers choose to do as soon as they arrive in Australia.

These 88 days include weekends if you are on a full-time basis, for example if you work from Monday to Friday 8 hours a day.

To be able to apply for this second visa, your employer must give you your salary slips (payslips) and fill in form 1263. You will have to sign this document.

Download your **1263 form** from the following link:
www.travellers.com.au/wp-content/uploads/2016/05/Evidence-of-Specified-Work-1263.pdf

Australian Government

Department of Immigration and Citizenship

Working Holiday visa: Employment verification

Form
1263

THIS IS NOT AN APPLICATION FORM

About this form

Important – Please read this information carefully before you complete your Employment verification. Once you have completed your Employment verification we strongly advise that you keep a copy for your records.

Who should use this form?

This form is for people who are in Australia as holders of a Working Holiday visa and who wish to apply for a second Working Holiday visa.

This form is to record details of employment in a specified field or industry in regional Australia.

Other evidence of specified work may include original or certified copies of payslips, group certificates, payment summaries, tax returns and employer references. Providing this evidence with this form will enable your application to be assessed more quickly.

The completed form should be retained and may be requested by the Department of Immigration and Citizenship (the department) after you lodge your application electronically to verify your specified work. If lodging a paper application, please attach this form.

To be eligible for a second Working Holiday visa, the applicant must have undertaken work for a minimum of 3 months (88 days in total) in a **specified field or industry*** in a designated area of **regional Australia****.

Specified work is any type of work in the list below:

- **plant and animal cultivation**:
  - cultivating or propagating plants, fungi or their products or parts;
  - general maintenance crop work;
  - harvesting and/or packing fruit and vegetable crops;
  - immediate processing of animal products including shearing, butchery in an abattoir, packing and tanning;
    Note: Secondary processing of animal products, such as small goods processing and retail butchery is not eligible.
  - immediate processing of plant products;
  - maintaining animals for the purpose of selling them or their bodily produce, including natural increase;
  - manufacturing dairy produce from raw material;
  - pruning and trimming vines and trees.

Eligible regional Australia postcodes

Regional areas	Postcodes
New South Wales (most areas except the greater Sydney area, Newcastle, the Central Coast and Wollongong)	2311 to 2312 2328 to 2411 2420 to 2490 2536 to 2551 2575 to 2594 2618 to 2739 2787 to 2898
Northern Territory	Entire Territory
Queensland (most areas except the greater Brisbane area and the Gold Coast)	4124 to 4125 4133 4211 4270 to 4272 4275 4280 4285 4287 4307 to 4499 4510 4512 4515 to 4519 4522 to 4899
South Australia	Entire State
Tasmania	Entire State
Victoria (most areas except the greater Melbourne area)	3139 3211 to 3334 3340 to 3424 3430 to 3649 3658 to 3749 3753, 3756, 3758, 3762, 3764 3778 to 3781 3783, 3797, 3799 3810 to 3909 3921 to 3925 3945 to 3974 3979 3981 to 3996
Western Australia (most areas except Perth and surrounding areas)	6041 to 6044 6083 to 6084 6121 to 6126 6200 to 6799

(Information about harvest work opportunities in regional Australia can be found at the Harvest Trail website at www.jobsearch.gov.au/harvesttrail)

Some vacancies on the Harvest Trail website may not be in the above eligible postcodes.

* For further information please see *'Specified work'* **www.immi.gov.au/visitors/working-holiday/417/ eligibility-second.htm**

** *'Regional Australia'* is restricted to areas within the postcodes listed in the opposite table.

- **fishing and pearling**:
  - conducting operations relating directly to taking or catching fish and other aquatic species;
  - conducting operations relating directly to taking or culturing pearls or pearl shell.

- **tree farming and felling**:
  - felling trees in a plantation or forest;
  - planting or tending trees in a plantation or forest that are intended to be felled;
  - transporting trees or parts of trees that were felled in a plantation or forest to the place where they are first to be milled or processed or from which they are to be transported to the place where they are to be milled or processed.

- **mining**:
  - coal mining;
  - construction material engineering
  - exploration;
  - metal ore mining;
  - mining support services;
  - oil and gas extraction;
  - other non-metallic mineral mining and quarrying.

- **construction**:
  - building completion services;
  - building installation services;
  - building structure services;
  - heavy and civil engineering construction;
  - land development and site preparation services;
  - non-residential building construction;
  - residential building construction;
  - other construction services.

Specified work:

- does not need to be paid work.
  Example: Work undertaken as a volunteer or through the Willing Workers on Organic Farms (WWOOF) scheme may also qualify if the work you undertook falls with the specified work definition above.

- does not need to be undertaken as a direct employee
  Example: Work in the list above as a contractor is eligible.

- must be listed above
  Example: Working as a nanny for a farmer would not be eligible.

Your personal details

1 Your full name as it appears on your passport

3 Your date of birth

DAY MONTH YEAR

2 Other names you are known by, if any
(including aliases, previous married names, names other than on your passport)

4 Your passport number

Your employment details

5 Details of employment in specified industries in regional Australia

You must keep a record of all dates worked. You will require this information when lodging your Working Holiday visa application electronically.

If you have worked for the same employer on more than one occasion, you should record each period of employment separately or attach a separate document containing these details.

If you have more employer details than will fit in the spaces below, attach a separate document containing these details.

You should attach evidence of your specified work (see page 1). This will allow your application to be assessed more quickly.

A *I confirm the following work has been undertaken*

Employee's full name

Type of work

Actual number of days worked

Start date DAY MONTH YEAR End date DAY MONTH YEAR Postcode where work was completed

Business name and address

Employer's telephone number ( )

Employer's full name

POSTCODE

Employer's ABN

Signature of employer

Name of contact for work verification *(eg. payroll officer/direct supervisor)*

E-mail address *(if available)* @

Contact person's telephone number ( )

B Employee's full name

Type of work

Actual number of days worked

Start date DAY MONTH YEAR End date DAY MONTH YEAR Postcode where work was completed

Business name and address

Employer's telephone number ( )

Employer's full name

POSTCODE

Employer's ABN

Signature of employer

Name of contact for work verification *(eg. payroll officer/direct supervisor)*

E-mail address *(if available)* @

Contact person's telephone number ( )

C Employee's full name

Type of work

Actual number of days worked

Start date DAY MONTH YEAR End date DAY MONTH YEAR Postcode where work was completed

Business name and address

Employer's telephone number ( )

Employer's full name

POSTCODE

Employer's ABN

Signature of employer

Name of contact for work verification *(eg. payroll officer/direct supervisor)*

E-mail address *(if available)* @

Contact person's telephone number ( )

D Employee's full name

Type of work

Actual number of days worked

Start date | DAY | MONTH | YEAR

End date | DAY | MONTH | YEAR

Postcode where work was completed

Business name and address

Employer's telephone number

( )

Employer's full name

Employer's ABN

Signature of employer

POSTCODE

Name of contact for work verification
(eg. payroll officer/direct supervisor)

E-mail address *(if available)*

@

Contact person's telephone number

( )

E Employee's full name

Type of work

Actual number of days worked

Start date | DAY | MONTH | YEAR

End date | DAY | MONTH | YEAR

Postcode where work was completed

Business name and address

Employer's telephone number

( )

Employer's full name

Employer's ABN

Signature of employer

POSTCODE

Name of contact for work verification
(eg. payroll officer/direct supervisor)

E-mail address *(if available)*

@

Contact person's telephone number

( )

Your contact details

6 Your e-mail address

7 Current residential address
(If applying in Australia, please give your current address in Australia)
Note: A post office box address is not acceptable as a residential address. Failure to give a residential address will result in your application being invalid.

POSTCODE

8 Address for correspondence
(This may be required by the department to communicate with you about your application. If the same as your residential address, write 'AS ABOVE')

POSTCODE

9 Your telephone numbers

Mobile

	COUNTRY CODE	AREA CODE	NUMBER
Office hours	(	) (	)
After hours	(	) (	)

Your declaration

WARNING: Giving false or misleading information is a serious offence.

10 *I declare that the information I have supplied on this form is complete, correct and up-to-date in every detail.*

Your signature

Date | DAY | MONTH | YEAR

We strongly advise that you keep a copy of your Employment verification and all attachments for your records.

Working conditions

You will have to leave your comfort zone and probably share some space with other people. In some cases, the owner hosts his employees on site and will deduct it from the salary slip.

Housing conditions are sometimes sketchy.

If you have your van, it's perfect because you're saving on housing.

It is also necessary to cop with the heat, the repetitive nature of the tasks and the weight of certain fruits, such as bananas for example.

Do not accept abusive working conditions.

For example, the prohibition of drinking or using the toilet for hours. When it is over 40 degrees all day long, you should drink 3-4 litres of water per day.

The salary

It varies from a region to another, meaning that you are often paid by the performance, by the basket (bucket or bin) or by the kilo, more rarely by the hour. This means that the faster you go, the more you earn.

This can be motivating for some, very discouraging for others.

If, for example, by doing your calculations, you earn less than AU\$21.6 an hour (the legal minimum), giving your maximum and it doesn't move in the following weeks, it's not a good plan.

Logically, you gain speed over the weeks, so your salary will follow. Some pickers reach AU\$200 a day. That's a great way to save money. If you want to be paid by the hour, opt for packing jobs (fruit packaging).

Beware of scams: working hostels and contractors

Many seasonal workers are fooled by the working hostels who promise you a job as *pickers* to sell you their accommodation.

Never pay in advance for accommodation. If you are asked for a deposit of AU$150 to work, run away!

Particular attention should be paid to the city of Bundaberg (Queensland), sadly renowned for these practices.

Not all working hostels are a scam. Some of them really offer work and provide decent accommodation.

The same applies to contractors who are an intermediary between the farm and you and who therefore take a commission.

In Victoria, many farms go exclusively through a contractor.

If you are asked to pay to apply for a job, go on your way. The best thing to do is to go directly to the site to prospect.

Some farms take advantage of the fact that you are in the middle of nowhere to sell you their accommodation.

Do I have to go to a working hostel if I don't have a car?

The advantage of a Working Hostel is that it can take you to your workplace every day. You leave with your team in the morning in a van and come back in the evening.

So YES, but always check the reviews on the Internet before you go there.

Sign an employment contract!

This may seem obvious, but it is important to remember it.
To get your second Working Holiday Visa and your 88 days, you will need your pay slips and contract.
Beware of farmers who say yes and make you wait on the spot until the fruit is mature.
Some are waiting for weeks on the spot, without pay of course. Check for yourself on the spot the condition of the fruit and if after 3 days you still do not start working, next!
If no contract, don't stay.

What to do in the event of a conflict with an employer?

In case of problems with a farm, contact **Fair Work Australia** to 13 13 13 94 (8am - 5.30pm Monday to Friday).

How to contact the farms ?

To contact the farms, you will have to call them, except for some who ask to apply online with a CV. First on the spot, first served. Don't wait until you're in the middle of the season to call, but anticipate!
"G'day! Are you looking for some pickers? »
If your English is not very good and you are in a van, or if you are several people in a car, you can go directly to the farm to ask them directly face to face if they are looking for some workers.
If you don't want to drive too far, the text messages work too!
If you call and the owner says ok on the phone, keep in mind that if another picker arrives before you, you will probably lose your chance.

The essentials

NEW SOUTH WALES

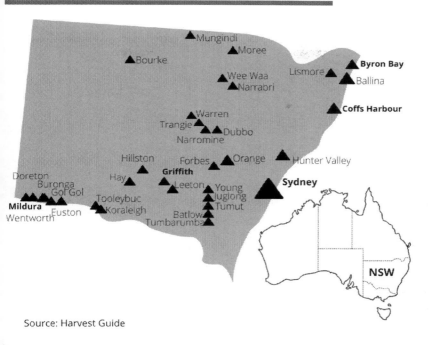

Source: Harvest Guide

Where to go depending on the season?

In Wentworth (1000 km West of Sydney) **high demand from May to August** for lemons (average demand in September), and **from February to September** for grapes (average demand in January). **October to November** for vegetables (average demand in January and February and between May and September).

In Young (374 Km West of Sydney) average demand for berries, grapes, and stonefruits from February to April, for cherries in November and December, and for plums between June and September.

Contact the farms even if the demand is not high.

In Wee Waa and Warren (600 km and 500 km North West of Sydney) **high demand from April to May** for cotton.

In Tumut (400 km South West of Sydney) **high demand between February and May** for apples.

In Tumbarumba (468 km South West of Sydney) **high demand from March to May** for apples (average demand for the rest of the year), **between February and April** for grapes (average demand between June and September), **between January and March** for berries (average demand in April and December).

In Trangie, average demand for cotton in April and May.

In Tooleybuc (895 km West of Sydney) **high demand between May and August and between October and January** for lemons (average demand in September), **between December and February** for stonefruit, **between February and April and from June to September** for grapes (average demand in January and May). Average demand between May and February for vegetables.

In the Sydney area, demand remains average all year round, from February to April for apples, avocados from December to February, August to November for lemons, November to January for stonefruit and all year round for vegetables, turf and flower nurseries.

In Orange (255 km West of Sydney) **high demand between February and April** for apples (average demand in May), **between February and April, and between June and September** for grapes (average demand in December), **November and December** for cherries (average demand in January).

In Narromine (430 km West of Sydney) **high demand in April and May** for cotton, **between May and October** for lemons (average demand between November and March).

In Narrabri and Mungindi (520 km and 748 km North West of Sydney) **high demand in April and May** for cotton (average demand in March in Mungindi).

In Moree (627 km North West of Sydney) **high demand in April and May** for cotton (average demand in March), **between May and July** for olives (average demand in April and August). Average demand between April and August for hazelnuts.

In Lismore (740 km North of Sydney) **high demand between June and October** for avocados (average demand in November), **between September and November** for berries (average demand in December, January, July and August), **in October and November** for stonefruits (average demand in December), **between May and July** for hazelnuts (average demand in April, August and September).

In Leeton (550 km West of Sydney) **high demand between October and March** for lemons (average demand throughout the rest of the year), **in February and March** for grapes, **between February and April and in November and December** for stonefruits (average demand in January). Average demand for vegetables between September and May.

In the Hunter Valley (240 km North of Sydney) **high demand in January and February and from June to August** for grapes (average demand in March and September).

In Hillston (680 km West of Sydney), **high demand in November** for cherries, **from October to February and from May to August** for lemons (average demand in March and April)**, from April to June** for cotton, **in July, August, November and December** for vegetables (average demand in June and September).

In Hay (720 km West of Sydney) **high demand between March and December** for vegetables. Average demand for melons between January and March, and for cotton in April and May.

In Griffith (570 km West of Sydney) **high demand between October and February and between June and August** for lemons (average demand in March, April, May and September), **between February and April and between June and August** for grapes (average demand in January), **between December and February** for vegetables (average demand in November and in March).

In Gol Gol (1000 km West of Sydney) **high demand between October and January and in June and July** for lemons (average demand in May, August and September)**, between February and April and between June and September** for grapes (average demand in January and May). Average demand for vegetables between May and February.

In Forbes (375km West of Sydney) **high demand between January and March** for stonefruits (average demand from October to December). Average demand from May to August for plums.

In Euston (920km East of Sydney) **high demand between February and April** for grapes (average demand in January and May), **and between May and September** for plums.
Average demand for vegetables between May and February.

In Dubbo (388 km West of Sydney) **high demand in April and May** for cotton.

In Coffs Harbour (524 km North of Sydney) **high demand between July and September** for avocados (average demand in June and between October and December), **between September and November** for berries (average demand in December, January, July and August). Average demand for bananas throughout the year.

In Byron Bay (763 km North of Sydney) **high demand in June and July** for avocados (average demand in April, May, August and September), **between September and November** for berries (average demand in July, August, December and January), **in February and March** for lychees, **between May and July** for hazelnuts (average demand in April, August and September). Average demand for stonefruits between September and December.

In Bourke (750 km North West of Sydney) **high demand between December and February and between May and September** for lemons, **in April and May** for cotton, **between November and January** for grapes (average demand in May and June), **from January to May** for melons, **in May and June** for plums.

In Batlow (440 km South West of Sydney) **high demand from March to May** for apples.

In Ballina (735 km North of Sydney) **high demand in June and July** for avocados (average demand in April, May, August and September), **between September and November** for berries (average demand in July, August, December and January) **and between May and July** for hazelnuts (average demand in April, August and September). Average demand for stonefruits between September and December.

High demand		▓▓		Average demand			░░				
	Jan.	Feb.	Mar.	April	May	June	July	Aug.	Sept.	Oct.	Nov.	Dec.
Ballina												
Batlow												
Bourke												
Byron Bay												
Coffs Harbour												
Dubbo												
Euston												
Forbes												
Gol Gol												
Griffith												
Hay												
Hillston												
Hunter Valley												
Leeton												
Lismore												
Moree												
Mungindi												
Narrabri												
Narromine												
Orange												
Sydney région												
Tooleybuc												
Trangie												
Tumbarumba												
Tumut												
Warren												
Wee Waa												
Wentworth												
Young												

Farm addresses and contacts

ORANGE

Harvest Information Service
1800 062 332   www.harvesttrail.gov.au

**Appledale Processors
Co-Operative Ltd.**
5 Stephen Pl, Orange NSW
02 6361 4422
www.appledale.com.au

Darley P R & J D
Daydawn, Nashdale NSW
02 6365 3278

Thornbrook Orchard (cherries)
39 Nashdale Ln, Nashdale
Paula : 04 27 269 437
www.thornbrookorchard.com.au
info@thornbrookorchard.com.au

Rossi Orchards Pty Ltd
98, Mount Pleasant La, Orange
02 6365 3106

Kirkwood J W Pty Ltd
Ballykeane, Orange NSW 2800
02 6362 9960

Pearce R S
Orange NSW 2800
02 63 65 82 16

**Huntley Berry Farm, Orange
non for profit disability
enterprise**
Huntley Rd, Huntley NSW
02 6365 5282
Mobile : 0427 252 308
www.huntleyberryfarm.com.au
huntleyberryfarm@octec.org.au
f www.facebook.com/huntleyberryfarm

D & J Vardanega Cherries
610 Pinnacle Road, Orange
02 6365 3242
wvardanega@gmail.com
f D & J Vardanega Cherries

Carinya Orchards Pty Ltd
98 Nancarrow La, Nashdale NSW
02 6365 3317

Gartrell David & Carolyn
"Wattleview"
Mt Lofty Rd, Nashdale NSW 2800
02 6365 3233

B Carthew
Towac Rd, Canobolas NSW 2800
02 63 65 31 38

Prudhomme P & A
Ku-Ring-Gai, Nashdale NSW 2800
📞 02 63 65 32 89

Cunich M E
Orange, Nashdale NSW 2800
📞 02 63 65 31 51

Huntley Berry Farm
Huntley Rd via, Orange NSW 2800
📞 02 63 65 52 82
✉ hurtleyberryfarm@otec.org.au
www.huntleyberryfarm.com.au
f www.facebook.com/huntleyberryfarm

Hillside Harvest
1209 The Escort Way Borenore
📞 02 6365 2247
www.hillsideharvest.com.au
f hillsideharvestorange

McClymont P A
Shed, Springside NSW 2800
📞 0418 350 163

Cunial G & T
Mount View, Nashdale NSW 2800
📞 02 6365 3187

BOURKE

Pitches R.G. & G. A.
Bourke NSW 2840
📞 02 68 72 22 67

Darling River Cotton Pty Ltd
Gorrell Ave, Bourke NSW
📞 0268 708521

NARROMINE

Mumblepeg
Mumble Peg, Narromine NSW 2821
📞 02 6889 6130

BYRON BAY / BALLINA

Blueberry Fields
769 Fernleigh Rd, Brooklet
📞 02 6687 8114
Call only on Wednesdays between 11am and noon. If there is no answer, it means that there is no more room. No email. Blueberry picking all year round with a high season between June and January. No accommodation on site.
www.blueberryfields.com.au

Byron Bay Organic Produce
Cnr Johnston Lane & Pacific Hwy, Ewingsdale
📞 02 6684 7007
Mobile: 0412865423
www.byronbayorganicproduce.com.au

Cape Byron Bush Foods
Lot 96/ Raywards La, Skinners Shoot
☎ 02 66 85 81 12

Aussie Orchards Growers & Packers
206 Warwick Park Rd, Mooball NSW
☎ 0421 381 129

Summerland Farm
253 Wardell Rd, Alstonville NSW
☎ 02 6628 0610
www.summerlandhousefarm.com.au

Ooray Orchards (35 min North of Byron Bay)- plums
28 Plumtree Pkt, Upper Burringbar
☎ 02 66 77 14 66

SYDNEY AREA

First Creek Wine Centre
McDonald Road Pokolbin NSW
☎ 02 4998 7293
✉ dstevens@firstcreekwines.com.au
or sales@firstcreekwines.com.au
www.firstcreekwines.com.au

Tyrrell's Wines
1838 Broke Rd, Pokolbin
☎ 01800 045 501
www.tyrrells.com.au

Gardiner B
Cornwallis, Windsor NSW 2756
☎ 02 4577 3231

Dtharowal Creek Nashi Orchard
Fountaindale Rd, Robertson
☎ 04 12 65 02 07

Apple Growers & Merchants Pty Ltd
Flemington NSW 2140
☎ 02 9746 8806

Cedar Creek Distributors
(100 km South of Sydney)
210 Mulhollands Rd, Thirlmere
☎ 02 46 81 84 57
www.cedarcreekorchards.com.au

Jerian Berry Pty Ltd
(140 km South of Sydney)
14 Kangaroo Valley Rd, Berry
☎ 04 08 25 86 16

Bakewell Graeme & Joanne
(316 km South of Sydney)
Peaches and nectarines
Mt George NSW 2424
☎ 02 65 50 65 13

Goddard K Stunt Farm
Mitchell Rd, Sackville North 2756
☎ 0245791 299

Summerfruit Australia

Apricots, nectarines, peaches and plums.
Main Rd, Mt George NSW 2424
☎ 03 93 29 21 00
✉ ceo@summerfruit.com.au
www.summerfruit.com.au

Montrose Berry Farm

Ormond St, Sutton Forest NSW
☎ 02 48 68 15 44
✉ info@montroseberryfarm.com.au
www.montroseberryfarm.com.au

Arcadia Orchard

(154 km South of Sydney)
Penrose NSW 2579
☎ 02 48 84 42 31
f www.facebook.com/arcadiaorchard

Wisbeys Orchards

(310 km South of Sydney)
Peaches and nectarines
LOT 1 Majors Creek Araluen Road,
Araluen NSW 2622
☎ 02 48 46 40 24

Batinich Barisha & Kathy

Rhodes NSW 2138
☎ 0263 843 221

GRIFFITH / LEETON

Aussie Gold Citrus

☎ 02 6963 6229
230 Slopes Rd, Tharbogang
f Aussie Gold Citrus

Fruitshack Farm

312 Henry Lawson Drive, Leeton
☎ 04 29 866 965

Warburn Estate

700 Kidman Way, Tharbogang
☎ 02 6963 8300
www.warburnestate.com.au
Check the job offers on the page
www.warburnestate.com.au/
vacancies
✉ info@warburnestate.com.au

Catania Fruit Salad Farm

187 Cox Rd, Hanwood NSW
☎ 04 27 630 219
www.cataniafruitsaladfarm.com.au

Bindera Orchard Pty Ltd

Farm 873/23 Aylett Rd, Stanbridge
☎ 02 69 55 29 00

Harvest Labour Assistance

MADEC Australia, Shop 3, 104 Yambil Street Griffith
☎ 1800 062 332   ✉ Griffith@madec.edu.au

Mia Vine Improvement Society Inc.
2655 Mallee Point Rd, Yenda NSW
📞 02 6968 1202
✉ miavis@bigpond.com

Hillyer P J (63 km South of Griffith)
Farm 1173, Yanco NSW 2703
📞 02 69 55 72 73

Mammarella D
Yenda NSW 2681
📞 02 69 68 11 86

Williams I J & M P
(40 km South of Griffith)
Stanbridge NSW 2705
📞 02 69 55 12 84

Auddino S & D
(50 km South of Griffith)
Farm 313, Wamoon NSW 2705
📞 02 69 55 94 30

NIANGALA

Koolkuna
144 Koolkuna Rd, Niangala NSW
📞 02 67 69 22 21/ 04 27 28 37 02
✉ koolkuna@ipstarmail.com.au
f Koolkuna-Berries

WENTWORTH

Scopelliti V
Curlwaa NSW 2648
📞 03 50 27 63 60

Medaglia J & J
Dareton NSW 2717
📞 03 50 27 45 96

Webley J
Channel Rd, Dareton NSW 2717
📞 03 50 27 45 38

Shepherd E G & M M
Boronia Crs, Dareton NSW 2717
📞 03 50 27 42 66

Clayson's
Silver City Hwy, Dareton NSW
📞 03 50 27 46 02

Stephens J M & S F
Boeill Creek NSW 2648
📞 0350 23 31 37

Lamshed R G
(50 km South of Wentworth)
Sturt Hwy, Monak NSW 2738
📞 03 50 24 02 12

Voullaire & Sons
Monak NSW 2738
📞 03 50 24 02 18

BATLOW

Pineview Orchard Pty Ltd

Kunama Via Batlow Ernis Way,
Batlow NSW

☏ 02 69 49 18 15
04 29 49 18 15
www.orchardpineview.com
f Orchard Pineview
✉ orchard_pineview@hotmail.com

HAY

Gravina Farms

Maude Rd, 2711
☏ 02 69934239

YOUNG

Hallmark Orchard

North Koepang P/L PO Box 1069
YOUNG NSW 2594
www.hallmarkorchards.com
Apply by email :
lucinda@hallmarkcherries.com.au

Big Cherry from Young

45 Richens La, Young NSW
☏ 0404 536 542 - 02 6382 1278
f The-Big-Cherry-from-Young
✉ the_big_cherry_young@hotmail.com

Anes Cherrygrove Orchard

Wombat Rd, Wombat NSW
☏ 0402 077 891

Valley Fresh Cherries and Stonefruits

4179 Olympic Hwy, South Young
☏ 02 63 84 32 21
www.valleyfreshcherries.com.au
✉ admin@valleyfreshcherries.com.au
f valleyFreshCherriesStonefruit

Eastlake's family tree

3923 Olympic Highway, Young
☏ 02 6384 3403
www.fairfieldsorchard.com.au
✉ admin@eastlakes.net

TOOLEYBUC

Hackett D N & J L

Goodnight NSW 2736
☏ 03 50 30 55 42

Wisbeys Orchards (peaches and nectarines)

LOT 1 Majors Creek Araluen Road,
Araluen NSW 2622
☏ 02 48 46 40 24

HILLSTON
Rennie Produce (Aust) Pty Ltd

Moora Farm Hillston, NSW 2675
☏ 02 6967 4152

31

TUMBARUMBA

Costa Group
Send your resume by email.
✉ employment.blueberry@costagroup.com.au
If no answer within 2 weeks , call
0266492784.

Uusitalo A
Courabyra NSW 2653
📞 02 69 48 86 29

Jolly Berries Blueberry Farm
(blueberries, raspberries, blackberries)
181 Wagga Rd, Tumbarumba NSW
📞 02 2 6948 2742
✉ jmcroz@westnet.com.au
www.jollyberries.com.au
f Jolly-berries-blueberries

HUNTER VALLEY

Popeye's Olive Farm
Luskintyre NSW 2321
📞 024930 6132

DUBBO

Bentivoglio Olives
(164 km East of Dubbo)
📞 0263 791 610
034 Tarmons Lue Rd, Rylstone
www.rylstoneolivepress.com.au
✉ rylstoneaustralianorganic@gmail.com
f www.facebook.com/rylstoneolivepress

WALLAROO
(300 km South of Sydney)

Loriendale Organic Orchard
(cherries, nectarines, peaches)
16 Carrington Rd,Wallaroo NSW
📞 02 62 30 25 57
✉ organics@loriendale.com.au
www.loriendale.com.au

FORBES

Girot Greg
Fairhaven, Forbes
📞 0458 287 628

Betland B A & M T
Bundaburrah NSW 2871
📞 02 68 53 22 40

Ellison R G (apples)
South Lead Rd, Forbes NSW
📞 02 6852 1704

Markwort F L (apples)
South Condobolin Rd, Forbes
📞 02 6852 1952

MOREE

T P Cotton
Moolahway, Manildra NSW
📞 02 6364 5025

Milo Cotton Co Farm Work
Milo, Moree NSW 2400
📞 02 6754 2147

Where to stay?

ORANGE

Check if the farm can accommodate you!

Federal Falls campground
Federal Falls Walking Track Canobolas
📞 02 6332 7640
npws.centralwest@environment.nsw.gov.au
www.nationalparks.nsw.gov.au
Free campsite.
10 sites available.
No booking possible.
First come, first served.

Canobolas Scout Camp
Lake Canobolas Rd, Nashdale
📞 02 6393 8000
www.nsw.scouts.com.au/groups/
✉ council@orange.nsw.gov.au
Fees apply.

Colour City Caravan Park
203 Margaret St, Orange
📞 02 6393 8980
www.orange.nsw.gov.au/contact/

BOURKE

Kidman's Camp
Mitchell Hwy, Bourke
📞 02 6872 1612
www.kidmanscamp.com.au
Book directly on the website.

Mitchell Caravan Park
2 Becker St, Bourke
📞 02 6830 0200
www.mitchellcaravanpark.com.au
✉ mcp1@outlook.com.au
From 25 AU$/night.

Yanda campground
Yanda Campground Trail,
Gunderbooka
📞 02 6393 8980
✉ npws.bourke@environment.nsw.gov.au
10 sites. 6 AU$/person

How to get to Orange?
256 km West of Sydney:
 + 19 AU$ - 34 AU$ (4h 45)
🚗 3h 40

How to get to Bourke?
800 km West of Sydney:
 73 AU$ (11h 30)
🚗 8h44

3?

NARROMINE / DUBBO

Narromine Rockwall Tourist Park

59 Mitchell Hwy, Narromine
📞 0437 656 594
www.narrominerockwalltouristpark.com.au
✉ narrominerockwall@gmail.com

Narromine Tourist Park & Motel

4108 Mitchell Hwy, Narromine
📞 02 6889 2129
✉ mail@narrominetouristpark.com.au
Between 15 AU$ and 30 AU$/night for the campsite.

Dubbo Holiday & Caravan Park

154 Whylandra Street, Dubbo
📞 02 6884 8633
✉ dubbo@discoveryparks.com.au
www.discoveryholidayparks.com.au
27-32 AU$ the campsite per night.

Dubbo Midstate Caravan Park

21 Bourke St, Dubbo
📞 02 6882 1155
https://dubbomidstate.com.au/
✉ dubbo@southerncrossparks.com.au
33 AU$ /night for camping

How to get there ?
400 km West of Sydney:
🚆 36 AU$ - 50 AU$ (6h30)
 5h

⚠ In Narromine and Dubbo
No local buses that go to the farms.
You should get a ride or arrange a pick-up from the station.

BYRON BAY / BALLINA

Backpackers Inn On The Beach

29 Shirley St, Byron Bay
📞 02 6685 8231
http://backpackersinnbyronbay.com.au/
✉ info@backpackersinnbyronbay.com.au
From 28 AU$/night in a dorm.

Wake Up! Byron Bay

25 Childe St, Byron Bay
📞 02 6685 7868
https://wakeup.com.au/
✉ askup@wakeup.com.au
From 41 AU$ the night in a dorm.

Reflections Holiday Parks Ballina

1 River St, Ballina
📞 02 6686 2220
www.reflectionsbookings.com.au
From 88 AU$ for the campsite for 2 nights.

Flat Rock Tent Park

38 Flat Rock Rd, East Ballina
📞 02 6686 4848
www.flatrockcamping.com.au
Between 36 and 48 AU$ per night for the campsite.

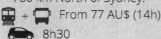

How to get there ?
766 km North of Sydney:
+ From 77 AU$ (14h)
 8h30

POKOLBIN / HUNTER VALLEY

Wine Country Tourist Park Hunter Valley
3 O'Connors Rd, Nulkaba
 02 4990 5819
https://winecountrytouristpark.com.au/
From 30 AU$ in low season, 35 AU$ in high season for the campsite.

McNamara Park (camping)
1273 Milbrodale Rd, Broke

How to get there?
164 km North of Sydney:
+ 41 AU$ - 56 AU$ (4h10)
 2h

GRIFFITH / LEETON

Griffith Caravan Village
 02 6962 3785
1 Gardiner Rd, Yoogali
www.griffithcaravanvillage.com.au
 reservations@griffithcaravanvillage.com.au

Oasis Caravan Park
 02 6953 3882
90 Corbie Hill Rd, Leeton

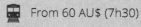

How to get there?
About 600 km from Sydney:
 From 60 AU$ (7h30)
 6h

WENTWORTH / GOL GOL

Willow Bend Caravan Park
 03 5027 3213
14-16 Darling St, Wentworth

Fort Courage Caravan Park
1703 Old Renmark Rd, Wentworth
 03 5027 3097

Rivergardens Holiday Park
Cnr Stuart Highway &, Punt Rd, Gol Gol
 03 5024 8541
www.rivergardensholidaypark.com.au
Campsite from 36 AU$/night.

How to get there?
About 1000 km from Sydney:
 80 to 109 AU$ (17h)
 From 270 AU$

Book your ticket (train and bus) on
www.transportnsw.info/regional

In Batlow ⚠
No local buses that go to the farms.
You should get a ride or arrange a pick-up from the station.

BATLOW

Batlow Caravan Park
Kurrajong Ave, Batlow
☎ 02 6949 1444
www.visitbatlow.com.au/161/775.ashx

Buddong Falls Campground
Hume and Hovell Walking Track, Buddong
☎ 02 6947 7025
www.nationalparks.nsw.gov.au
Free campsite.

The Apple Inn (motel)
1 Tumbarumba Rd, Batlow
☎ 02 6949 1342
https://www.appleinn.com.au/
✉ reception@appleinn.com.au
Consider this option if you are 2 people to share a room at 94 AU$/night.

HAY

Hay Big 4 (camping)
☎ 02 6993 1875
4 Nailor St, Hay
www.big4.com.au
Between 25 and 45 AU$/night

How to go to Hay ?
725 km West of Sydney:
 + From 81 AU$ (12h15)
🚗 (8h25)

YOUNG

Young Tourist Caravan Park
17 Edwards St, Young
☎ 02 6382 2190
www.youngcaravanpark.com.au
✉ youngtouristpark@gmail.com
Campsite from 33 AU$/night.

Boorowa Caravan Park
93 Brial St, Boorowa
☎ 02 6385 3658
www.visitnsw.com/destinations

How to get there?
374 km West of Sydney:
 + From 54 AU$ (7h52)
🚗 (4h)

How to get there?
About 400 km from Sydney:
 + 65 AU$ (9h12)
 🚗 (4h30)

In Tooleybuc ⚠
No local buses that go to the farms. You should get a ride or arrange a pick-up from Swan Hill station.

TOOLEYBUC

Tooleybuc Pet Friendly Caravan Park
63 Murray St, Tooleybuc
📞 03 5030 5025

Tooleybuc Country Roads Motor Inn
78 Cadell St, Tooleybuc
📞 03 5030 5401
www.tooleybuccountryroads.com.au
If you are 2 people to share a room at 90 AU$.

How to get there?
900 km West of Sydney:
🚌 100 - 193 AU$ (15h)
🚗 (9h10)

HILLSTON

Billabourie Riverside Tourist Park
Mt Grace Road, (Wallanthry Road), Hillston
📞 0427 674 131

Willandra group campground
📞 02 6966 8100
Yinnagalang Billana Track, Roto
www.nationalparks.nsw.gov.au
6 AU$/person/night.

How to get to Hillston ?
682 km West of Sydney:
no local buses
🚗 (7h16)

TUMBARUMBA

Tumbarumba Creek Caravan Park
Lauder St, Tumbarumba
📞 02 6948 3330

Buddong Falls Campground
Hume and Hovell Walking Track, Buddong
📞 02 6947 7025
www.nationalparks.nsw.gov.au/
Free campsite. No booking.
First arrived, first served.

How to get there?
470 km South West of Sydney:
🚆 + 🚌 From 68 AU$ (9h48)
🚗 (5h)

37

FORBES

BIG4 Forbes Holiday Park

141 Flint St, Forbes
☏ 02 6852 1055
www.big4.com.au/caravan-parks/
Campsite from 26 to 49 AU$ /night.

Apex Riverside Tourist Park

88 Reymond St, Forbes
☏ 02 6851 1929

How to get there?
386 km West of Sydney:

🚆 + 🚌 From 44 AU$ (6h43)
🚗 (4h45)

**To find a campsite, download the application WIKICAMPS
www.wikicamps.com.au**

NORTHERN TERRITORY

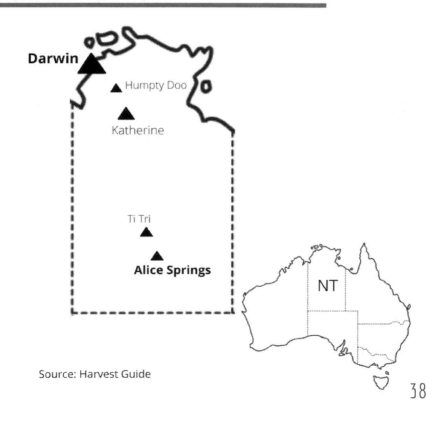

Source: Harvest Guide

Where to go depending on the season?

In Darwin, high demand from September to November for mangoes. Average demand between August and October for melons.
In Katherine, high demand from October to December for mangoes. Average demand for melons from May to November and for vegetables from May to October.

					High demand				Average demand			
	Jan.	Feb.	Mar.	April	May	June	July	Aug.	Sept.	Oct.	Nov.	Dec.
Darwin								▒	▓	▓	▓	
Katherine					▒	▒	▒	▒	▒	▓	▒	▓

Farm addresses and contacts

DARWIN

Pearl farms
(All year round with a peak from April-May to September-October). The salary is about 150 AU$/day. Careful, this job isn't for everyone. You have to cop with the heat, the fishy smells and the hours.
You may be asked to start at 4:00 in the morning.
You'll soon be covered in mud, of sea water, starting in the morning and for the next ten hours.

Paspaley Pearls
📞 08 8982 5560
✉ recruitment@paspaley.com.au
www.paspaleygroup.com

Fruit picking

Middle Point Farm Pty Ltd
(tropical fruits)
GPO Box 2511, Darwin NT 0801
📞 08 89 83 25 55

Southport Siding Exotic Fruit Farm (70 km South of Darwin)
Lot 4, Head Of Cavenagh, Duddel Rd, Darwin River Dam NT 0822
📞 08 89 88 60 66

Milkwood Tropical Orchards
(100 km South of Darwin)
Mangoes, avocados, lemons
Batchelor NT 0845
📞 04 09 32 54 99
www.milkwoodtropical.com.au

Acacia Hills Farm PTY Ltd

(63 km South of Darwin)
Mangoes
31 Golding Rd, Acacia Hills NT
☏ 08 89 88 14 67

Jabiru Tropical Orchards (50 km

South of Darwin)- Tropical fruits.
5 Hopewell Rd, Berry Springs NT
☏ 08 89 88 61 50

The Melon patch

(45 km from Darwin)- Melons
1015 Pioneer Drv, Humpty Doo NT
☏ 08 99 88 19 87

Sweet Life

(55 km East of Darwin)
255 Alphatonia Rd, Lambells
Lagoon NT 0822
☏ 08 99 88 19 99

Tropiculture Australia

(30 km from Darwin)-
Limes, tropical fruits.
110 Horne Rd, Bees Creek NT 08
☏ 08 99 88 11 1
f Tropiculture Australia

Cdml Ellis Enterprises

(340 km South of Darwin)
470 Cossack Rd, Florina NT 0852
☏ 08 89 72 24 82

KATHERINE

Manbulloo Mangoes Australia Pty Ltd

Victoria Hwy, Katherine NT 0850
☏ 08 89 72 25 90
www.manbulloo.com
You can send your resume to
✉ employment@manbulloo.com

ALICE SPRINGS

Rocky Hill Table Grapes

Undoolya Station Alice Springs NT
✉ rockyhillmagic@bigpond.com

TI TREE

(200 km North of Alice Springs)

Red Centre Farm (mangoes)

Stuart Hwy, Ti Tree NT 0872
☏ 08 89 56 98 28
✉ ognam@bigpond.com.au

The Desert Fruit Company

NT Portion 7016, Deepwell
via Alice Springs NT
☏ 08 89 56 07 82
✉ info@desertfruitcompany.com.au
sales@desertfruitcompany.com.au
www.desertfruitcompany.com.au

Table Grape Growers Of Australia

Mail Bag 88, Alice Springs NT 0872
☏ 08 89 56 97 44

40

Where to stay ?

Check if the farm can accommodate you!

DARWIN

Youth hostels are of very average quality in Darwin.

Melaleuca On Mitchell (MOM)
Dormitory: From 26 AUD$.
52 Mitchell Street Darwin
📞 08 8941 7800/ 1300 723 437
www.momdarwin.com
From 55 AUD$ the double room or twin.

The best is to share a twin in a hotel for more comfort.

Argus Hotel Darwin
13 Shepherd St, Darwin City
📞 08 8941 8300
From 76 AU$/night for a twin.
https://argusaccommodation.com.au/
✉ reservations@argushotel.com.au

Darwin City Hotel
59 Smith St, Darwin City
📞 08 7981 5125
www.darwincityhotel.com/
✉ stay@darwincityhotel.com
From 69 AU$/night for a double room.

Coconut Grove Holiday Apartments
146 Dick Ward Dr, Coconut Grove
📞 08 8985 0500
From 65 AU$/night
www.coconutgroveapartments.com.au

KATHERINE

Pine Tree Motel
3 Third St, Katherine
📞 08 8972 2533
Twin from 69 AU$/night.
www.pinetreemotel.com.au
✉ reservations@pinetreemotel.com.au

Riverview Tourist Village
(camping)
440 Victoria Hwy, Katherine
📞 08 8972 1011
www.riverviewtouristvillage.com.au
✉ info@riverviewtouristvillage.com.au
40-45 AU$/night for a campsite.

How to get there?
317 km South of Darwin
🚌 From 78 AU$ (4h)
🚗 (3h20)

Book your bus ticket directly on
www.greyhound.com.au/book-a-ticket/availability

4.

ALICE SPRINGS

Youth hostels in Alice are pretty good.

Alice's Secret Travellers Inn
Dormitory: From 26 AUD$.
Twin room from 65 AU$.
6 Khalick St, East Side NT
📞 08 8952 8686
www.asecret.com.au
✉ stay@asecret.com.au

Jump Inn Alice Budget Accommodation
Dormitory: From 26 AUD$.
Twin room from 77 AU$.
4 Traeger Ave, The Gap NT
📞 08 8929 1609
www.jumpinnalice.com
✉ stay@jumpinnalice.com

Alice Lodge Backpackers
Dormitory: From 25 AUD$/night
Twin room from 63 AU$/night
4 Mueller St, East Side NT
📞 08 8953 1975
https://alicelodge.com.au
✉ info@alicelodge.com.au

Alice Springs YHA
Dormitory: From 29 AUD$.
Twin room from 95 AU$.
Cnr Parsons Street and, Leichhardt Terrace, Alice Springs
📞 08 8952 8855
www.yha.com.au/
✉ alicesprings@yha.com.au

Alice Springs Tourist Park
70 Larapinta Dr, Araluen
📞 08 8952 2547
www.alicespringstouristpark.com.au
✉ info@alicespringstouristpark.com.au
25-39 AU$/night for a campsite.
From 95 AU$/night for a double cabin.

Wintersun Cabin & Caravan Park
Crn. Stuart Highway and Head Street, Alice Springs
📞 08 8952 4080
www.wintersun.com.au
✉ wintersun@wintersun.com.au
From 43 AU$/night for a campsite.

How to get there?
1500 km South of Darwin
🚌 From 212 AU$ (21h35)
🚗 (16h20)
✈ From 300 AU$

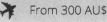

QUEENSLAND

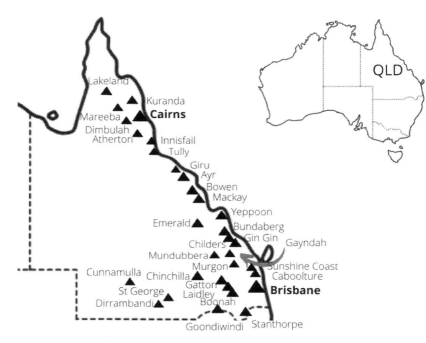

Source: Harvest Guide

Where to go depending on the season?

Around Cairns

In Tully (140 km South of Cairns), **high demand all year round** for bananas.

In Innisfail (88 km South of Cairns), **high demand all year round** for bananas.

In Lakeland (250 km North of Cairns) **high demand all year round** for bananas.

In Atherton (95km South West of Cairns), **high demand from March to May** for avocados (average demand in February and in June), **from April to June** for apples (average demand in March and in July) and for vegetables from October to December (average demand in September).
Average demand all year around for bananas.

In Ayr (435km South of Cairns on the coast), **high demand between May and November** for vegetables, **in November and December** for mangoes, **in May and June, then between September and December** for melons.
Average demand for tomatoes between May and November.

In Bowen (550km South of Cairns on the coast), **high demand between September and November** for melons (average demand in May and June), **in December** for mangoes (average demand in November and in January), **between May and November** for tomatoes.
Average demand between May and November for vegetables.

In Dimbulah (113 km West of Cairns), **high demand in December and January** for mangoes (average demand in November).
Average demand from February to April for avocados, from November to April for vegetables, from November to March for lychees.

In Giru (400 km South of Cairns), **high demand in November and December** for mangoes. Average demand from May to November for vegetables.

In Mareeba (60 km West of Cairns), **high demand in February and March** for avocados (average demand in April and May), **in December and January** for mangoes (average demand in February, March and November).

Average demand all year around for bananas and lemons, between November and March for lychees, between October and February for pineapple and between April and September for vegetables.

Around Brisbane

In Bundaberg (360 km North of Brisbane), average demand for avocados between April and August, between March and July for lemons. **High demand between May and July** for macadamia (average demand in March, April, August and September), **in January and February** for mangoes (average demand in December), **from September to November** for melons (average demand in May and June), **from April to August and from October to December** for tomatoes (average demand in September), **from April to December** for vegetables. Average demand all year around for berries.

In Gayndah (324 km North West of Brisbane), **high demand between April and August** for lemons (average demand in September and between November and March), **between June and August** for avocados (average demand in September and October.

In Boonah (86km South West of Brisbane), **high demand between November and April** for tomatoes, **between December and February** for melons. Average demand all year around for vegetables.

In Dirranbandi (600 km West of Brisbane), average demand between March and May for cotton.

In Emerald (870 km North West of Brisbane), **high demand between May and July** for lemons (average demand in March, April, August and September), **in November and December** for grapes (average demand in May, June and October) **and in September and October** for melons (average demand between April and August and in November and December).
Average demand for cotton between March and May.

In Childers (310 km North of Brisbane), **high demand in February** for mangoes (average demand in January and March), **in November and December** for vegetables (average demand in October).
Average demand for avocados from July to April, for lemons from March to July, for lychees from December to February and for tomatoes from April to September.

In Gatton (92 km West of Brisbane), **high demand between September and June** for vegetables (average demand in July and August), **in December** for melons (average demand in January and February). Average demand for tomatoes between November and May.

In Gin Gin (347 km North of Brisbane), **high demand between March and May** for lemons (average demand between December and February), **in January and February** for mangoes (average demand in March and April).
Average demand from February to September for avocados, from January to March for dragon fruits and from April to October for vegetables.

In Goondiwindi (350 km West of Brisbane), average demand between March and May for cotton.

In Laidley (86 km West of Brisbane), **high demand all year around** for vegetables, **from December to February** for melons.
Average demand from November to May for tomatoes.

In **Mundubbera** (360 km North West of Brisbane), **high demand** for lemons (average demand in April, August and September), **in December** for grapes (average demand in June, July and November), **in January** for mangoes.

Average demande for berries between August and November.

In **St George** (500 km West of Brisbane), **high demand between December and March** for grapes (average demand between June and November), **between December and March** for melons (average demand in April and in November), **between October and December** for vegetables.

Average demand between March and June for cotton.

In **Stanthorpe** (218 km South West of Brisbane), **high demand between February and April** for apples and pears (average demand from November to January and in May), **in November and December** for stonefruits (average demand in September and in October), **from January to April** for tomatoes (average demand in May and in December), **from November to March** for vegetables (average demand in April, May and October), **from February to April and in November and December** for strawberries (average demand in January, May and October).

In **Chinchilla** (300 km West of Brisbane), **high demand in December and in April** for melons (average demand from January to March). Average demand in November for vegetables.

In **Caboolture** (50 km North of Brisbane), **high demand between July and October** for strawberries (average demand between March and June and in November), **between March and June** for pineapples (average demand in February, September, October and November), **between May and August** for raspberries (average demand in April).

In **Cunnamulla** (800 km West of Brisbane), **high demand in December and January** for grapes (average demand in May, June, July, September and October).

CALENDAR OF SEASONS | QUEENSLAND

In Sunshine Coast (100 km North of Brisbane), **high demand between August and October** for strawberries (average demand in March, April, July and November). Average demand between April and June for apples, in February, March and May and then between August and October for ginger, between February and May and then in September and October for pineapples.

In Yeppoon (655 km North of Brisbane), average demand in January and February for mangoes, in November and January for lychees, in March and April for apples and between January and March for pineapples.

High demand	░░		Average demand	░░							

	Jan.	Feb.	Mar.	April	May	June	July	Aug.	Sept.	Oct.	Nov.	Dec.
Atherton												
Ayr												
Boonah												
Bowen												
Bundaberg												
Caboolture												
Childers												
Chinchilla												
Cunnamulla												
Dirranbandi												
Emerald												
Gatton												
Gayndah												
Gin Gin												
Giru												
Goondiwindi												
Innisfail												
Laidley												
Lakeland												
Mareeba												
Mundubbera												
Stanthorpe												
St George												
Sunshine Coast												
Tully												
Yeppoon												

Farm addresses and contacts

BRISBANE

Qld Citrus (lemons)
Southgate Commercial Cntr/ 250 Sherwood Rd, Rocklea QLD 4106
📞 073379 3833

Farm Fresh Central
25 Sperling St, Rocklea QLD 4106
📞 07 32 16 65 07

Qld Citrus Growers Incorporate
(lemons)
250 Sherwood Rd, Rocklea QLD
📞 07 33 79 38 33

Randall's Farm Fresh Fruit & Vegies
Birkdale Rd, Birkdale QLD 4159
📞 07 32 07 25 09

CAIRNS

Jonsson's Farm Market
31 Johnston St, Stratford QLD 4870
📞 07 40 58 90 00
www.jonssonsfarmmarket.com.au
f Jonsson's Farm Market

Scomazzons Roadside Stall
(77 km North of Cairns)
Scomazzon Rd,Mossman QLD 4873
📞 07 40 98 34 46

Scomazzons Roadside Stall
(77 km North of Cairns)
Scomazzon Rd,Mossman QLD
📞 07 40 98 34 46

Rainforest Pawpaws
(71 km South of Cairns)
Price Rd, Bartle Frere QLD
📞 07 40 67 64 17

Vanilla Australia
(67 km North of Cairns)
Captain Cook Hwy, Port Douglas
📞 07 40 99 33 80
✉ info@vanillaaustralia.com
or VanillaAustralia@Gmail.com
www.vanillaaustralia.com

Crystal Brook Exotic Farm
(112 km North of Cairns)
Stewarts Creek Rd, Daintree QLD
📞 07 40 98 62 72

Blushing Acres (apples)
66027 Burke Development Rd, Dimbulah QLD 4872
📞 07 40 93 51 55
f BlushingAcres
(Apply by message Facebook).

MAREEBA

Bellview Orchards (avocados)
155 Rains Road, Mareeba
📞 04 0823 1363

Top Of The Range Lychee
(58 km North of Mareeba)
RP 908 Rex Highway, Julatten
📞 07 40 94 13 45

Golden Triangle Avocado
(29 km South of Mareeba)
Kimmins Rd, Tolga QLD 4882
📞 07 4095 4381

Avocado Estates
 (29 km South of Mareeba)
535 Beantree Rd, Tolga QLD
📞 07 4095 4587

Rigato Farms Pty Ltd
Kennedy Highway, 4880 Mareeba
📞 07 4093 3555

TULLY

Lissi M A
Mullins Rd, Tully QLD 4854
📞 07 4066 7980

Dores Bananas
(23 km South of Tully)
Dores Road (4854) Murray Upper
📞 07 4066 5561

Chiquita North Queensland
Syndicate Rd, Tully QLD
📞 074066 7945

Pinnacle Hill Lychees
402 Pinnacle Hill Rd, Toobanna
📞 07 47 77 22 77
✉ cjb.phl@lycheesaustralia.com.au
www.lycheesaustralia.com.au/

Collins Farms
8 Bamber St, Tully QLD 4854
📞 07 4068 1268
f Collins-Banana-Farm

G&J Flegler PTY LTD
LOT 1 Davidson Rd, Euramo
📞 07 4066 7577

CNC Banana Co.
798 Davidson Rd, Euramo QLD
📞 07 4066 7810

Dundee Creek Banana
Bruce Hwy, Tully QLD 4854
📞 0740682770

GIN GIN

McMahon Citrus Pty Ltd
Abbotsleigh, Wallaville QLD
📞 07 41 57 61 70

Monduran Citrus
3245 Monduran Rd, Gin Gin
📞 07 4157 3816

Abbotsleigh Citrus
251 Grahams Rd, Gin Gin
📞 07 4157 6980
www.abbotsleigh.com.au
✉ abbotsleighadmin@nutrano.com.au

GAYNDAH / MUNDUBBERA

Robinson A G
Humphrey Binjour Rd, Gayndah
📞 0741 61 19 55

Burnett Valley Olive Growers Association Inc
(140 km South of Gayndah)
PO Box 382, Kingaroy QLD
📞 07 41 62 58 56

Zipf N & Sons
Glenrae Dip Rd, Mundubbera
📞 07 41 65 43 77

Trott B J & J E & Sons
(38 km West of Gayndah)
Coonambula Rd, Mundubbera
📞 07 41 65 47 55

Gr8 Citrus Pty Ltd (lemons)
196 Mt Lawless Rd, Gayndah
📞 07 41 61 15 32

Two Pine Orchard
Bonaccord Rd, Gayndah QLD
📞 07 41 61 22 85
f Two Pine Orchard

Riverton Orchard (lemons)
Gayndah QLD 4625
📞 07 41 61 61 73

Quebec Orchard
Mundubbera QLD 4626
📞 07 41 65 61 39

Glen Grove Orchard (lemons)
Boomerang Rd, Gayndah QLD
📞 07 41 61 11 96
✉ admin@glengrove.com.au

Auburnvale Citrus Pty Ltd
(lemons)
Hawkwood Rd, Derri Derra QLD
📞 07 41 65 61 65

Ventnor Grove Pty Ltd (lemons)
Coonambula Rd, Mundubbera
📞 07 41 65 43 60

Glenellen Pty Ltd (lemons)
Humphrey Binjour Rd, Gayndah
📞 07 41 61 19 55

Murray & Averial Benham
«Benyenda», Gayndah QLD
📞 07 41 61 62 49

GIRU / AYR /TOWNSVILLE

R&M Packing
(55 km North of Townsville)
19 Hencamp Creek Rd.Rollingstone
📞 07 47707430

Paradise Estate Produce
27 Lisa Drv, Ayr
📞 0747 834 585

Davco Farming
(24 km West of Ayr)
484 Pelican Rd , Ayr
📞 07 4782 7575
✉ office@davcofarming.com
www.davcofarming.com

Bugeja Cane Farm
Old Clare Rd, Ayr QLD 4807
📞 07 4783 1984

A&JO Felesina
Leibrecht Rd, Airville QLD 4807
📞 07 4782 6869

Ace Mangoes
(82 km North of Ayr and
8 km from Townsville)
14 Tomkins St, Cluden QLD 4811
📞 07 4778 1672

Penruth Produce (tomatoes)
123 Queen St, Ayr QLD 4807
📞 07 4783 6169

Ollera Tropical Orchards
(111 km North of Giru)
Ponderosa Rd, Rollingstone QLD
📞 07 47 70 81 82

BOWEN

Battiston F & Co
Bruce Highway, Gumlu
📞 0747 848 161

Elphinstone & Kirby Pty Ltd
"Leslie", Mt Dangar QLD 4805
📞 07 4785 2244

GATTON

Gatton Fruit Bowl (tomatoes)
Spencer St, Gatton QLD 4343
📞 07 5462 1435

Windolf Farms Pty Ltd
671 Mount Sylvia Rd, Upper Tenthill
www.windolffarms.com.au
To apply, call between 8am and
4pm from Monday to Friday:
📞 07 5462 6121.

Rugby Farm Pty Ltd
22 Hoods Rd, Gatton QLD
📞 07 5466 3200
www.rugbyfarm.com.au
Apply directly on the link :
www.rugbyfarm.com.au/employme
nt.html

Kesteven Farms (44 km West of
Gatton and 8km from Toowoomba)
Toowoomba QLD4350
📞 07 46 30 14 68

Blackboy Ridge
385 Forestry Rd, Vinegar Hill QLD
📞 07 5462 5202
f blackboyridge

Kiwi Land Orchard
Keys Rd, Hampton QLD 4352
📞 07 46 97 91 68

Wodonga Park Fruit & Nuts
(avocados, madadamia)
45 Mt. Binga Road, Mt. Binga QLD
📞 07 41 63 01 66 (Guy Butler)
✉ wpfn@mail.com
www.wodonga-park.com.au

Bauer's Organic Farm Pty Ltd
1166 Mount Sylvia Rd, Mt Sylvia
hwww.bauersorganic.com
Do not call but only apply via the
form here:
www.bauersorganic.com/get-in-
touch

YEPPOON

Wilson's Paw Paws-Papayas
(30 km South of Yeppoon)
Sleipner Rd, Tungamull QLD
📞 07 49 34 42 34

Gemkid (43 km South West of
Yeppoon and 3 km from
Rockampton)
10 Craigilee St, The Range QLD
📞 07 49 27 00 68

**Talorb Pty Ltd T/A Tropical
Pines**
Rockhampton Rd, Yeppoon QLD
📞 07 49 39 57 49

Keppel Orchards (apples, avocados, mangoes, lemons)
414 Keppel Sands Road, Keppel Sands
📞 0438 307 011
f Keppel Orchards

CABOOLTURE

Hermes Strawberries Pty Ltd (strawberries)
490 Newlands Rd, Wamuran
📞 0422 333 071
www.hermesstrawberries.com.au
Apply directly on the website
http://hermesstrawberries.com.au

Sunray Strawberries
347 King Rd, Wamuran QLD 4512
📞 07 5496 7364
✉ admin@sunraystrawberries.com.au
f www.facebook.com/SunrayStrawberry

Schiffke Pty Ltd. (strawberries)
210 Stern Rd, Bellmere QLD
📞 07 5495 8274
f TSLFAMILYFARMS

R G & R J Forster (apples)
24 km North of Caboolture.
160 Judds Rd, Glass House Mountains QLD 4518
📞 07 54 96 91 29

Piñata Farms
382 Scurr Rd, Wamuran QLD
📞 07 5497 4295
✉ info@pinata.com.au
Apply directly on the page
www.pinata.com.au

Berry Patch farm (strawberries)
Lot 1 O Shea Rd, Wamuran QLD
📞 07 54 96 68 80

Stothart Family Farms
219 Stern Rd, Bellmere, QLD 4510
📞 07 54 95 87 95
https://stothart.wordpress.com/

SUNSHINE COAST

Koogie Downs Strawberry Farm
58 Rainforest Road, Chevallum
📞 07 5445 9100
✉ brsdaniels@iprimus.com.au

Harvest information Service
📞 1800 062 332
www.harvesttrail.gov.au

Sunfresh Pines (70 km West of Sunshine Coast)
Tunnel Rd, Kandanga QLD 4570
☎ 07 5484 3269 / 0419 774 384
✉ sunfresh@spiderweb.com.au
www.sunshinecoastregionalfood.com.au

All About Fruit New Farm
(105 km South of Sunshine Coast)
85 Merthyr Rd, New Farm QLD
☎ 07 33 58 63 44
www.allaboutfruitandjuice.com.au/
f www.facebook.com/AllAboutFruit

Kandanga Farm (70 km North-West of Sunshine Coast)
93 Main St, Kandanga QLD 4570
☎ 07 5484 3771
www.kandangafarmstore.com.au
f Kandanga-Farm-Store

Avocado Australia Ltd
U8/ 63 Annerley Rd,
Woolloongabba QLD 4102
☎ 07 38 46 65 66
✉ admin@avocado.org.au
www.avocado.org.au

Harvest information Service
☎ 1800 062 332
www.harvesttrail.gov.au

Sunshine Coast Farm
133 Laxton Rd, Palmview
☎ 07 54 94 51 46
✉ info@strawberryfields.com.au
www.strawberryfields.com.au
f StrawberryfieldsAustralia

Eumundi Strawberry Farm
(strawberries)
Strawberry La, Eumundi QLD
☎ 07 54 42 82 13
✉ eumundistrawberries@bigpond.com
f Eumundi-Strawberry-Picking

STANTHORPE

Tornabene E A
(11 km South of Stanthorpe)
Glen Aplin, QLD 4381
☎ 07 46 83 43 33

Patane Transport
«Wallaroo Orchards», Severnlea
☎ 07 46 83 52 54

Geoff Farrelly & Sons
(17 km North of Stanthorpe)
Border Gate Rd, Cottonvale QLD
☎ 07 46 85 22 25

A R Allan
173 Kelly Rd, Applethorpe QLD
☎ 07 46 83 22 54

Ballandean Estate Wines
(20 km South of Stanthorpe)
354 Sundown Rd, Ballandean QLD
☎ 07 4684 1226
✉ info@ballandeanestate.com

W Mann
Emu Swamp Rd, Glen Aplin QLD
☎ 07 46 83 43 08

Fast Fruit Sales
Amiens Rd, Thulimbah QLD
☎ 07 46 85 21 91

Bent & Haynes Pty Ltd
Ballandean QLD 4382
☎ 07 46 84 11 56

Sunstate Fruits Pty Ltd
285 Border Rd, Applethorpe QLD
☎ 07 46 83 24 22

Volpato A & W
Newlands Rd, Cottonvale QLD
☎ 07 46 85 22 20

A Baronio
113 Matthews La, The Summit
☎ 07 46 83 22 86

A & A Gangemi
154 Goodwin Rd, The Summit
☎ 07 46 83 23 25

Brisotto I & R (apples)
21 Ann St, Applethorpe QLD 4378
☎ 07 46 83 22 93

Belvedere Orchard
Quirks Rd, Amiens QLD 4352
☎ 07 46 83 32 08

P Savio
Savio La, Pozieres QLD 4352
☎ 07 46 85 33 12

A Filipetto
Amiens Rd, Pozieres QLD 4352
☎ 07 46 85 32 09

C Andreatta
Andreatta La, Pozieres QLD 4352
☎ 07 46 85 32 53

A & I Nicoletti
61 Nicoletti La, Pozieres QLD 4352
☎ 07 46 85 32 31
✉ admin@nicolettiorchards.com.au
www.nicolettiorchards.com.au
f www.facebook.com/nicolettiorchards

T R & A M Carnell
Back Creek Rd, Severnlea QLD
☎ 07 46 83 53 65

G & J Mattiazzi (apples)
Halloran Drv, Cottonvale QLD
📞 07 46 85 22 06

BOONAH

Peak Crossing Pawpaw Farm
(28 km North of Boonah)
Washpool Rd,Peak Crossing QLD
📞 07 54 67 20 30
f Peak-Crossing-Pawpaw-Farm

Telemon Orchards (50 km
South of Boonah) - lemons
1 Philp Rd, Rathdowney QLD
📞 07 55 44 12 32

Kalfresh
6206 Cunningham Hwy, Kalbar
📞 07 5463 7290
www.kalfresh.com.au
✉ info@kalfresh.com.au
Send your resume to Karl
(specifying your visa) :
karl@kalfresh.com.au
f Kalfresh Vegetables

Harvest information service
📞 1800 062 332
www.harvesttrail.gov.au

CHILDERS

Simpson Farms Pty Ltd
Goodwood Plantation Goodwood
Rd, Childers QLD
📞 07 41 26 82 00
✉ admin@simpsonfarms.com
www.simpsonfarms.com.au
(For applications, fill the form
directly on the website)

Sunstate Orchards (86 km South
of Childers) - Lemons
Tiaro QLD 4650
📞 07 41 29 25 03

Campbell Partnership
Dallarnil QLD 4621
📞 07 41 27 72 33

BUNDABERG

Mission Beach Bananas
(bananas)
1023 Ten Mile Rd, Sharon QLD
📞 07 41 57 70 14

MacLennan I
(50 km West of Bundaberg)
Bruce Hwy, Wallaville QLD 4671
📞 07 41 57 62 36

FARM ADDRESSES AND CONTACTS | QUEENSLAND

Eden Farms (cucumber)
324 Dahls Road, Bundaberg
📞 07 41 59 76 09
✉ manager@edenfarms.com.au
www.edenfarms.com.au
f edenfarmsaustralia
Apply between November and March
by phone or via this form
www.edenfarms.com.au/employment

Bundaberg Fruit & Vegetable Growers
Unit 13 2 Tantitha St, Bundaberg
📞 07 41 53 30 07
✉ bfvg.info@bfvg.com.au
www.bfvg.com.au
Kylie Jackson Agriculture
Workforce Officer
📞 Mob: 0488 533 801
✉ kylie.jackson@bfvg.com.au

Spencer Ranch Pty Ltd
(lemons)
50 km West of Bundaberg.
97 McLennan Drv, Wallaville
📞 07 41 57 62 45

Basacar Produce (apples)
4551 Goodwood Rd, Alloway
📞 07 41 59 78 89

Harvest Informations
📞 1800 062 332
www.harvesttrail.gov.au

INNISFAIL

Wadda Plantation
(22km West of Innisfail)
Pullom Rd, Nerada QLD 4860
📞 0740 645 233 (call to apply)
www.waddabananas.com.au/

Pacific Coast Produce
228 Boogan Rd, Innisfail QLD
📞 0740 642 452
✉ info@eco-banana.com.au
www.eco-banana.com.au

Brighton Banana Farm
787 East Feluga Rd, East Feluga
📞 07 4068 2215

Australian Banana
101 Upper Daradgee Rd, Upper Daradgee QLD
📞 07 4061 6833
LinkedIn :
https://www.linkedin.com/company/australian-banana-company-pty-ltd-?originalSubdomain=fr

Hampson Bros
(23 km West of Innisfail)
565 Mount Utchee Creek Rd, Utchee Creek QLD 4871
📞 07 4065 3382

58

Rigoni Bros (Bananas)
22 km West of Innisfail
📞 0740 645 181
Gattera Rd Nerada QLD 4860

Robson K G (bananas)
Flying Fish Point Rd, Innisfail
📞 07 4061 4632

Alcock Bananas
645 Palmerston Hwy, Innisfail
📞 07 4061 2971

Fresh Yellow Bananas
291 Boogan Rd, Boogan QLD
📞 07 4064 3000
f Fresh-Yellow

Tropicana Banana
445 Upper Daradgee Rd, Upper
Daradgee QLD 4860
📞 02 9746 8348
www.tropicanabanana.com.au
Gavin Eilers: 0447005166
Chris Rummary: 0497013260
For the farm in Mareeba :
Scott Franklin: 0438794667

Gonzos Bananas
Bruce Hwy, Mourilyan QLD 4858
📞 07 4063 2451

Ask your free PDF in color by email
contact@helpstage.com

Where to stay?

Check if the farm can accommodate you

BRISBANE

Summer House Backpackers Brisbane
Dormitory: From 22 AUD$/night
350 Upper Roma St, Brisbane City
📞 07 3236 5007
www.staysummerhouse.com
✉ brisbane@staysummerhouse.com

Brisbane City YHA
Dormitory: From 35 AUD$/night
Twin room from 97 AU$/night
392 Upper Roma St, Brisbane City
📞 07 3236 1004
www.yha.com.au
✉ brisbanecity@yha.com.au

Bowen Terrace Accommodation
Dormitory: From 24 AUD$/night
Twin room from 66 AU$/night
365 Bowen Terrace, New Farm
📞 07 3254 0458
www.bowenterrace.com.au
✉ book@bowenterrace.com.au

Breeze Lodge
Dormitory: From 33 AUD$/night
635 Main St, Kangaroo Point
📞 07 3156 8434
www.breezelodge.com.au
✉ stay@breezelodge.com.au

CAIRNS

Gilligan's Backpacker Hotel & Resort Cairns
Dormitory: From 15 AUD$/night
57-89 Grafton St, Cairns City
📞 07 4041 6566
www.gilligans.com.au
✉ reservations@gilligans.com.au

Mad Monkey Backpackers Village
Dormitory: From 18 AUD$/night
Double room from 61 AU$/night
141 Sheridan St, Cairns City
📞 07 4231 9612
www.madmonkey.com.au
✉ village@madmonkey.com.au

Summer House Backpackers Cairns
Dormitory: From 13 AUD$/night
Twin room from 55 AU$/night
341 Lake St, Cairns City
📞 07 4221 3411
hwww.staysummerhouse.com
✉ cairns@staysummerhouse.com

MAREEBA

Camp Paterson (camping)
540 Shanty Creek Rd, Mareeba
📞 0428 030 885
www.camppaterson.com.au
✉ info@camppaterson.com.au

Riverside Caravan Park
13 Egan St, Mareeba
📞 07 4092 2309

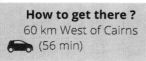
How to get there ?
60 km West of Cairns
🚗 (56 min)

TULLY

Jackaroo Treehouse Mission Beach (29 km from Tully)
13 Frizelle Rd, Bingil Bay
📞 07 4210 6008
Dormitory: From 24 AUD$/night
Double room from 62 AU$/night
www.jackarootreehouse.com
✉ info@jackarootreehouse.com

Dunk Island View Caravan Park (camping)
21-35 Webb Rd, Wongaling Beach
📞 07 4068 8248
From 36 AU$/night for the campsite.
www.dunkislandviewcaravanpark.com
✉ info@dunkislandviewcaravanpark.com

How to get to Tully ?
140 km South of Cairns
🚌 From 29 AU$ (2h30)
🚗 1h50

GAYNDAH / MUNDUBBERA

Riverside Carvan Park
11-15 Dalgangal Rd, Gayndah
📞 07 4161 1911
www.riversidegayndah.com
✉ riversidegayndah@gmail.com
From 26 AU$/night for a campsite

Mundubbera Three Rivers Tourist Park
37 Strathdee St, Mundubbera
📞 07 4165 3000
www.threeriverspark.com.au
✉ admin@threeriverspark.com.au

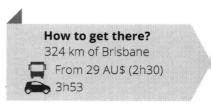
How to get there?
324 km of Brisbane
🚌 From 29 AU$ (2h30)
🚗 3h53

Civic Guesthouse
262 Walker St, Townsville
📞 07 4771 5381
Dormitory: From 21 AUD$/night
Twin from 52 AU$/night
www.civicguesthousetownsville.com.au
✉ info@civicguesthouse.com.au

Orchid Guest House

34 Hale St, Townsville
☎ 0418 738 867
www.orchidguesthouse.com.au/
✉ fames@bigpond.net.au
Dormitory: From 24 AUD$/night
Twin room from 56 AU$/night

Discovery Parks - Townsville

6 University Rd, Wulguru
☎ 07 4778 4555
www.discoveryholidayparks.com.au
From 30 AUD$/night for the
campsite.

> **How to get there?**
> 347 km South of Cairns
> 🚌 From 58 AU$ (4h45)
> 🚗 4h07
> ✈ From 140 AU$ (1h) with
> Qantas or Rex

GIN GIN

Gin Gin Hotel

Twin room from 79 AUD$ /night
(to share)
66 Mulgrave St, Gin Gin
☎ 07 4157 2106

> **How to get there?**
> 347 km North of Brisbane
> 🚌 From 113 AU$ (7h20)
> 🚗 4h

GATTON

Heifer Creek (camping)

2536 Gatton Clifton Rd, Fordsdale

Lake Dyer Caravan & Camping Ground

134 Gatton Laidley Rd E, Laidley
Heights
☎ 07 5465 3698

> **How to get there?**
> 92 km West of Brisbane
> 🚌 From 26 AU$ (1h10)
> 🚗 1h10

YEPPOON

Yeppoon Beachhouse

58 Farnborough Rd, Yeppoon
☎ 07 4910 5264
Dormitory: From 28 AUD$/night
Twin room from 80 AU$/night
www.yeppoonbeachhouse.com.au

Beachside Caravan Park

45-51 Farnborough Rd, Yeppoon
☎ 07 4939 3738
www.beachsidecaravanparkyeppoon.com.au

> **How to get there?**
> 655 km North of Brisbane
> 🚆 From 71 AU$ (10h39)
> 🚗 7h36

BOWEN

Tropical Beach Caravan Park
25 Argyle St, Bowen
☎ 07 4785 1490
From 32 AU$/night for the campsite.
www.tropicalbeachcaravanparkbowen.com.au
✉ info@tropicalbeachcaravanparkbowen.com

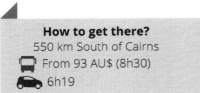

How to get there?
550 km South of Cairns
🚌 From 93 AU$ (8h30)
🚗 6h19

CABOOLTURE

Highland House
Twin room from 70 AUD$ (to share)
277 Victoria Ave, Redcliffe
☎ 0416 233 502

How to get there?
52 km North of Brisbane
🚆 From 7 AU$ (47 min)
🚗 45min

SUNSHINE COAST

Noosa Flashpackers
Dormitory from 38 AUD$/night
102 Pacific Ave, Sunshine Beach
☎ 07 5455 4088
www.flashpackersnoosa.com

BIG4 Caloundra Holiday Park
(camping)
44 Maloja Ave, Caloundra
☎ 01800 550 138
https://big4caloundra.com.au/
✉ enquiry@big4caloundra.com.au

Cotton Tree Holiday Park
Cotton Tree Parade, Cotton Tree
☎ 07 5459 9070
www.sunshinecoastholidayparks.com.au
From 43 AU$/night for the campsite.

How to get there?
105 km North of Brisbane
🚆 From 23 AU$ (2h25)
🚗 1h18

STANTHORPE

Sommerville Valley Tourist Park
63 Sommerville Ln, Stanthorpe
☎ 07 4681 4200
www.sommervillevalley.com.au
✉ info@sommervillevalley.com.au
From 30 AU$/night for the campsite.

Book your bus ticket directly on
www.greyhound.com.au

Country Style Caravan Park

27156 New England Hwy, Glen Aplin
 07 4683 4358
www.countrystylecaravanpark.com.au
From 35 AU$/night for the campsite.

How to get to Stanthorpe ?
218 km South West of Brisbane
From 55 AU$ (2h39)
2h38

BOONAH

Frog Buttress

https://qpws.usedirect.com/qpws/
Mount French QLD
0137468

You can book accommodation in Boonah by contacting the Boonah Visitor Information Centre.
 07 5463 223

How to get there?
86 km South West of Brisbane
 1h

CHILDERS

Childers Tourist Park & Camp

11 Stockyard Rd, North Isis
07 4126 1371
www.childerstouristparkandcamp.com.au
chilltourpark@gmail.com
Prices on request.

Iron Ridge Park (camping)

1472 Goodwood Rd, Redridge
07 4126 8410
www.ironridgepark.com.au
admin@ironridgepark.com.au
From 28 AU$/night for the campsite.

How to get there?
310 km North of Brisbane
From 95 AU$ (7h)
3h32

BUNDABERG

Bunk Inn Hostel

Dormitory from 32 AU$/night.
25 Barolin St, Bundaberg Central
0497 055 350
www.bunkinnhostel.com.au
contact@bunkinnhostel.com.au

Palms Hostel

Dormitory from 28 AU$/night.
7 Bauer Street, 4670 Bargara
Reservations directly on
www.booking.com

How to get there?
360 km North of Brisbane
From 97 AU$ (7h)
7h-9h

SOUTH AUSTRALIA

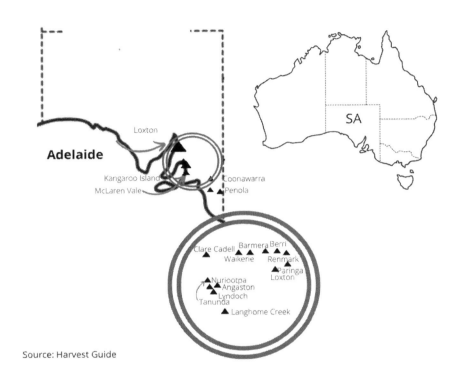

Source: Harvest Guide

Where to go depending on the season?

In Adelaide Hills (30 km from Adelaide), average demand from February to May for apples and pears, November to January for cherries, February to April and June to December for grapes.

In Angaston (88 km North of Adelaide), **high demand in February, March, July, August, October and November** for grapes (average demand in April, June, September and December).

6

In Barmera (227 km East of Adelaide), **high demand in October and November** for cherries, **between June and November** for lemons (average demand between December and February and in May), **in February, March, June and July** for grapes (average demand in January, April and August), **between November and February** for stonefruits (average demand in March and in October).

In Berri (240 km East of Adelaide), **in Cadell** (185 km North East of Adelaide), **in Paringa** (260 km East of Adelaide), **in Renmark** (257 km from Adelaide), **and in Waikerie** (180 km East of Adelaide) **high demand between June and November** for lemons (average demand between December and February and in May), **in February, March, June and July** for grapes (average demand in January, April and August), between November and February for stonefruits (average demand in March and October).

In Clare 140 km North of Adelaide) **and in Langhorne Creek** (64 km South East of Adelaide), **high demand in February, March, July and August** for grapes (average demand in April, June and September).

In Coonawarra (373 km South of Adelaide), **high demand from December to February and in April and May** for vegetables (average demand in March and June), **in December and January** for cherries, **from February to August** for grapes.

In Loxton (256 km East of Adelaide), **high demand from January to March** for apples (average demand in avril and in December), **from February to April** for grapes (average demand in January and between June and August), **between June and November** for lemons (average demand from December to February and in May).
Average demand for stonefruits between October and March.

In Lyndoch (59 km North East of Adelaide), high demand between February and April for grapes (average demand between June and December).

In **Lyndoch** (59 km North East of Adelaide), **high demand between February and April** for grapes (average demand between June and December).

In **McLaren Vale** (40 km South of Adelaide), **high demand in March, June and July** for grapes (average demand in February, April, May and August).

In **Nuriootpa and in Tanunda** (80 km and 75 km North East of Adelaide), **high demand in February, March, July, August, October and November** for grapes (average demand in April, June, September and December).

In **Penola** (382 km South of Adelaide), **high demand between December and June** for vegetables, **in December and January** for cherries, **between February and August** for grapes.

High demand		Average demand										
	Jan.	Feb.	Mar.	April	May	June	July	Aug.	Sept.	Oct.	Nov.	Dec.
Adelaide Hills												
Angaston												
Barmera												
Berri												
Cadell												
Clare												
Coonawarra												
Langhorne Creek												
Loxton												
Lyndoch												
McLaren Vale												
Nuriootpa												
Paringa												
Penola												
Renmark												
Tanunda												
Waikerie												

Farm addresses and contacts

WIRRABARA / BEETALOO VALLEY (100 km North of Clare, 245 km from Adelaide)

Curtis N A
Wirrabara SA 5481
📞 08 86 68 41 70

Beetaloo Grove (olives)
Beetaloo Gr, Beetaloo Valley SA
📞 0418 844 935
✉ enquiries@beetaloogrove.com.au
www.beetaloogrove.com.au

LANGHORNE CREEK

Thomson J P & J G (50 km from Langhorne Creek)
North Bokara Rd, Mypolonga
📞 08 85 35 41 94

WAIKERIE

Miller D K & M M
Waikerie SA 5330
📞 08 85 43 22 56

Frankleigh Fruits
Carter Rd, Waikerie SA
📞 08 85 41 22 96

Sunlands Produce
Sunlands SA 5322
📞 08 85 41 90 28

Boehm M W & D A
Ramco SA 5322
📞 08 85 41 35 76

Wurst A C (lemons)
72 D Channel Rd, Waikerie SA
📞 08 85 41 20 18

G M Arnold & Son Pty Ltd
Waikerie SA 5330
📞 08 85 41 20 91

Travaglione Q
Waikerie SA 5330
📞 08 85 41 25 29

Red Earth Farms (melons, grapes, lemons, hazelnuts)
PMB 10 Waikerie SA 5330
📞 Stephen : (04) 28 41 91 18
✉ info@redearthfarms.com
www.redearthfarms.com

DeVito A D & P E
Waikerie SA 5330
📞 04 27 41 24 52

Liebich David L
Morgan-Renmark Rd,Taylorville
📞 08 85 43 22 57

Camerlengo A A
D Channel Rd, Waikerie
📞 08 85 41 29 67

Wurst A C
72 D Channel Rd, Waikerie SA
📞 08 85 41 20 18

Ohlmeyer K E & H A & B K
Sturt Hwy, Waikerie SA
📞 08 85 40 50 50

Noble Gregory J
Sunlands SA 5322
📞 08 85 41 90 57

L & R citrus Pty Ltd (lemons)
Lewis Rd, Waikerie SA 5330
📞 08 85 41 24 70

Murray View Irrigation Pty Ltd
Murray View Rd, Qualco SA 5320
📞 08 85 41 90 37

Jubilee Almonds (hazelnuts)
13923 Goyder Highway WAIKERIE
📞 08 85 89 30 38
✉ brendan@jubileealmonds.com

Ricciuto M A & C (lemons)
Waikerie SA 5330
📞 08 85 41 26 70

ADELAIDE AREA

Varverakis C & M
(40 km North of Adelaide)
129 Gawler River Rd, Lewiston
📞 08 85 24 33 42

Magarey AA & Sons
(16 km South of Adelaide)-
plums, pears and apples.
40 Magarey Rd Coromandel Valley
📞 08 82 78 10 34
www.magareyorchard.com
f magareyorchard
✉ admin@magareyorchard.com

Cottonville Farms
(24 km South of Adelaide)
1 Kanbara Rd West, Scott Creek
📞 08 83 88 25 25

Drury Orchards (30 km East of
Adelaide)- apples and pears.
Inglewood SA 5133
📞 08 83 80 54 21

Walkers International
(36 km East of Adelaide)
24 Blaser Road, MYLOR, SA 5153
📞 08 83 88 53 90
www.walkerfamilyfarms.com.au

69

Smith Gully Orchards

(15 km East of Adelaide)
Cherries, apples, lemons, etc.
49 Smiths Gully Rd, Montacute
📞 08 83 90 22 65
✉ smithgullyorchards@ihug.com.au
www.smithgullyorchards.com.au
f Smith-Gully-Orchards

Montacute Valley Orchards

(cherries, stonefruits, lemons, etc)
Institute Rd, Montacute SA 5134
📞 08 83 90 22 13
✉ sales@montacutevalleyorchards.com.au
ou montacute.valley.orchards@gmail.com
www.montacutevalleyorchards.com.au
f MontacuteValleyOrchards

PENOLA

Penola Strawberry Farm

(strawberries, apples)
Church St, Penola SA 5277
📞 08 87 37 29 66

MCLAREN VALE

Blueberry Hill-Glaetzer's

(blueberries)
182 Peel Rd, Pages Flat SA
📞 08 85 56 12 04

The Blueberry Patch (blueberries

from December to February)
36 km South of McLaren Vale
558 Nangkita Rd, Mt Compass SA
📞 08 85 56 91 00
✉ farm@blueberrypatch.com.au
www.blueberrypatch.com.au
f The-Blueberry-Patch/

Fleurieu Cherries (cherries)

19 km South of McLaren Vale.
159 Pages Flat Rd, Pages Flat, S.A.
📞 08 85 56 13 14
✉ info@fleurieucherries.com
www.fleurieucherries.com
f www.facebook.com/farmcherries

CADELL

Apold S & H Pty Ltd

PMB 85, Morgan SA 5320
📞 08 85 40 40 53

Rob & Karen Smyth

Cadell SA 5321
📞 08) 85 40 32 08

Walker C A & P A

Ramco Rd, Ramco SA 5322
📞 04 85 41 41 00

Harvest Labour Assistance
8 Ral Ral Avenue Renmark SA
📞 1800 062 332 ✉ renmark@madec.edu.au

Leske M R & P A
Ramco SA 5322
📞 08 85 41 26 05

ADELAIDE HILLS

MacDonald Fruit
Powell Rd, Kersbrook SA 5231
📞 08 83 89 32 03

HarrisVille Orchards
(cherries, apples)
Harris Rd, Lenswood SA 5240
📞 0407 427 747
www.harrisvilleorchards.com
✉ harrisvilleorchards@bigpond.com
f Harrisville-Orchards

Verrall S M Para Dell
(25 km North of Adelaide Hills)
Verrall Rd, Upper Hermitage
📞 08 83 80 52 76

Drury Orchards Pty Ltd
(19 km North of Adelaide Hills)
Paracombe Rd, Inglewood SA
📞 08 83 80 53 01

K & R Filsell & Sons
(apples, pears)
Deviation Rd, Forest Range SA
📞 08 83 89 82 49

Appelinna Hills
Plummers Rd, Forest Range SA
📞 08 83 89 84 13
✉ appelinnahills@gmail.com
www.appelinnahills.com.au

LL Dearman & Sons
Paracombe SA 5132
📞 08 83 80 52 78

Paracombe Premium Perry
169, Murphy Rd, Paracombe
📞 0402 082 532
www.paracombepremiumperry.
com.au
f ParacombePremiumPerry
✉ info@paracombepremiumperry.com.au

Aberdeen Orchards
Tiers Rd, Lenswood SA 5240
📞 08 83 89 84 29

I L & K L Plummer
(apples, pears)
Hewlett Rd, Lenswood SA 5240
📞 08 83 89 82 38

Hillview Fruits NPL
Main Rd, Lenswood SA 5240
📞 08 83 89 82 97

Harvest Labour Assistance MADEC Australia
📞 1800 062 332 ✉ mountbarker@madec.edu.au

Plummers Border Valley Orchards Pty Ltd
Jackson Hill Rd, Gumeracha SA
📞 08 83 89 11 24
Ian : 0407.716.929,
Gavin : 0407.898.318
www.cherry-picking.com.au
(possibility to contact them by message via the form on their site).

Hillview Fruits NPL
(apples, pears)
Main Rd, Lenswood SA 5240
📞 08 83 89 82 97

Bower Berries
Lot 9 Edward Hill Rd, Lenswood
📞 08 83 89 81 93

BARMERA / RENMARK

Cordaro N & R
Tapalin St, Renmark SA 5341
📞 08 85 95 13 23

Tassios T & T
Renmark Ave, Renmark SA
📞 08 85 95 14 26

Harvest Labour Assistance
8 Ral Ral Avenue Renmark SA
📞 1800 062 332
✉ renmark@madec.edu.au

Johnson T E & L J
510 Cobdogla, Barmera SA 5345
📞 04) 17 81 42 19

Recchia L
Gallery Tce, Lyrup SA 5343
📞 08 85 83 82 16

Babaniotis G
Twenty-Fourth St, Renmark SA
📞 08 85 86 68 49

Richards A R
Renmark Ave, Renmark SA 5341
📞 08 85 95 13 07

Ekonomopoulos B & C (lemons)
Cooltong Ave, Renmark North SA
📞 08 85 95 31 69

Sims P G & S D
Bookmark Ave, Renmark West SA
📞 08 85 95 16 18

Klingbiel T W & J E
Barmera SA 5345
📞 08 85 88 71 55

B A B S Harvesting & Contracting Pty Ltd
Culgoa St, RENMARK NORTH SA
📞 08 85 95 30 27

Martinko J
Renmark SA 5341
📞 08 85 95 50 46

Hoffman V R & P L (apples)
Hoffman Rd, Barmera SA 5345
📞 08 85 88 20 84

Beech A G & J A
Cnr Thelma & Evans Rds, Barmera
📞 08 85 88 20 38

Levak F & K
Barmera West SA 5345
📞 08 85 88 70 16

Reed J M
Barmera SA 5345
📞 08 85 88 28 79

Edmonds Rick
Main Rd, Cooltong SA
📞 08 85 95 72 17

Hausler K C
Lot 6/ Hd Renmark I D Renmark
West SA
📞 08 85 95 13 17

Mason Brian R
Barmera SA 5345
📞 08 85 88 31 61

Gallo Orchards Pty Ltd
Lot 9/ Ral Ral Ave Renmark North
📞 08 85 95 35 55

Johnson K L & V D
PO Box 76, Moorook SA 5332
📞 08 85 84 90 84

Rapisarda A & M
Moorook SA 5332
📞 08 85 83 92 70

Kypreos A
Mcintosh Ave, Glossop SA 5344
📞 04 19 51 43 52

Kondoprias S & M
Berriman Rd, Monash SA 5342
📞 08 85 83 55 66

Liakos A & A
Trenaman Rd, Monash SA 5342
📞 08 85 83 53 72

Frahn I H
Lobban Rd, Monash SA 5342
📞 08 85 83 53 26

Kollias J & S
Section 804 McKenzie Rd, Loveday
📞 08 85 83 94 00

DelZoppo A R & P G
321 Hunt Rd, Loveday SA 5345
📞 08 85 88 71 25

Dimou John & Son
Warrego St,Renmark North SA
📞 08 85 95 32 83

A Sourtzis Fruit Growers
Twentysixth St, Renmark West SA
📞 04 38 08 53 73

Grant L W
Teal St, Renmark North SA
📞 08 85 95 33 24

Mystere Orchards
Main Rd, Cooltong SA
📞 08 27 95 72 29

Nobile S
Monash SA 5342
📞 08 85 83 53 73

Edmonds Rick
Main Rd, Cooltong SA
📞 08 85 95 72 17

LOXTON / BERRI

Lawrie R F & M C
Sturt Hwy, Berri SA 5343
📞 08 85 82 14 69

Nagy L & V
Winkie SA 5343
📞 08 85 83 72 62

Lippis T & T
Sykes Rd, Lyrup SA 5343
📞 08 85 83 82 62

Ruediger Bill & Pam
Loxton SA 5333
📞 08 85 82 15 96

Jaeschke D E & J A
Loxton SA 5333
📞 08 85 82 11 29

Brand A J & K L
Brand Drv, Berri SA 5343
📞 08 85 82 29 43

Swanbury A E & M J
Loxton SA 5333
📞 08 85 84 47 69

Lloyd L D & Sons Pty Ltd
Pike Creek Rd, Lyrup, SA 5343
📞 08 85 83 83 48

Wegener C L & B J
Trenamin Rd, Glossop SA 5344
📞 08 85 83 20 64

Plush John & Julie
Winkie SA 5343
📞 08 85 83 73 07

Lindner P R
McKay Rd, Loxton East SA 5333
📞 08 85 84 69 45

74

Pipinis D
Sturt Hwy, Berri SA 5343
📞 08 85 82 14 80

Panagopoulous I
Gratwick Rd, Loxton East SA
📞 04 85 84 69 64

Jaeschke D E & J A
Loxton SA 5333
📞 08 85 82 11 29

Googee
62 Powell St, Berri SA
📞 08 85 82 18 96

Biddle B R & M A
Cutler Rd, Loxton North SA 5333
📞 08 85 84 12 77

Weaver R A & M K
Balfour-Ogilvy Ave, Loxton North
📞 08 85 84 12 42

Cottee Harold W Pty Ltd
1086, Murtho Rd, Murtho SA
📞 08 85 95 80 43

Gillainey Orchards (lemons)
Lot 58 Murtho Rd Paringa,
📞 08 85 95 52 51
f Gillainey-Orchards

NURIOOTPA

Munzberg & Co Pty Ltd
Research Rd, Tanunda SA 5352
📞 04 18 39 68 41

Kerrsbrook Cherry Farm
(cerises)
Kersbrook Rd, Kersbrook SA 5231
📞 08 83 89 22 31

Permedah Pty Ltd
Paringa SA 5340
📞 08 85 95 50 34

Pike River Produce (grapes)
Loxton Rd, Paringa SA 5340
📞 08 85 95 50 10

Harvest information Service
📞 1800 062 332
www.harvesttrail.gov.au

Where to stay ? Check if the farm can accommodate you

WIRRABARA / BEETALOO VALLEY

Ippinitchie Camp Grounds
Wirrabara SA 5481
www.parks.sa.gov.au

How to get there?
241 km North of Adelaide
🚌 From 124 AU$ (3h20)
🚗 2h45

ADELAIDE

Adelaide Central YHA
135 Waymouth St, Adelaide
Dormitory from 37 AU$/night
📞 08 8414 3010
www.yha.com.au
✉ adlcentral@yha.com.au

Tequila Sunrise Hostel
23 Waymouth Street, Adelaide
📞 0451 434 627
Dormitory from 23 AU$/night
http://tequilasunrisehostel.com
✉ admin@tequilasunrisehostel.com

Backpack Oz
144 Wakefield St, Adelaide
📞 08 8223 3551
Dormitory from 24 AU$/night
http://backpackoz.com.au/

The Guest House
144 Wakefield Street (Cnr of Pulteney & Wakefield Street), Adelaide
Dormitory from 25 AU$/night
📞 08 8223 3551
http://backpackoz.com.au

Hostel 109 Flashpackers
109 Carrington St, Adelaide
📞 08 8223 1771
Dormitory from 31 AU$/night
www.hostel109.com
✉ stay@hostel109.com.au

WAIKERIE

Waikerie Holiday Park
44 Peake Terrace, Waikerie
📞 08 8541 2651
https://waikerieholidaypark.com.au
✉ stay@waikerieholidaypark.com.au
From 36 AU$/night for the campsite.

How to get there?
184 km East of Adelaide
🚌 From 30 AU$ (2h40)
🚗 2h06

PENOLA

Coonawarra Bush Holiday Park

242 Comaum School Rd, Comaum

📞 0455 146 647

https://cbhp.com.au/

✉ slm@cbhp.com.au

How to get there?
382 km South of Adelaide

🚌 From 60 AU$ (5h38)

🚗 4h

MCLAREN VALE

McLaren Vale Lakeside Caravan Park

48 Field St, McLaren Vale

📞 08 8323 9255

www.mclarenvalelakesidecaravanpark.com.au

✉ mclarenvalelakeside@bigpond.com

From 34 AU$/night for the campsite.

How to get there?
40 km South of Adelaide

🚆 From 7 AU$ (1h37)

🚗 40 min

CADELL

Commercial Hotel Morgan

13 Railway Terrace, Morgan

📞 08 8540 2107

www.commercialhotelmorgan.com/

✉ commercialhotelmorgan@outlook.com

From 45 AU$/night for a twin.

How to get there?
189 km North East of Adelaide

🚌 From 39 AU$ (4h13)

🚗 2h11

ADELAIDE HILLS

Adelaide Brownhill Creek Tourist Park

60 Brown Hill Creek Rd, Adelaide

📞 01800 626 493

www.brownhillcreekcaravanpark.com.a

✉ info@brownhillcreekcaravanpark.com.au

From 29 AU$/night for the campsite

Shiloh Hills Park

354 Pole Rd, Ironbank SA

📞 0428 661 802

www.shilohills.com.au/

From 15 AU$/night/person for the campsite.

YHA camp ground

Mount Crawford SA

📞 08 8521 1700

www.forestrysa.com.au

Cromer Shed

Mount Crawford SA

www.forestrysa.com.au

📞 08 8521 1700

7

How to get to Adelaide Hills?
40 km East of Adelaide
 From 4 AU$ (20 min)
 39 min

BARMERA / RENMARK

Kingston-on-Murray Caravan Park
461 Holmes Rd, 5331 Kingston on Murray
📞 08 8583 0209
www.komcaravanpark.com.au
✉ info@komcaravanpark.com.au
From 55 AU$/night for a bungalow.

Riverbend Caravan Park
01 Sturt Hwy, Renmark
📞 08 8595 5131
www.riverbendrenmark.com.au
✉ stay@riverbendrenmark.com.au
From 44 AU$/night for the campsite.

BIG4 Renmark Riverfront Holiday Park
Sturt Hwy, Renmark
📞 08 8586 8111
https://big4renmark.com.au
✉ stay@big4renmark.com.au
From 46 AU$/night for the campsite.

How to get to Barmera ?
261 km East of Adelaide
 From 40 AU$ (4h)
 3h08

LOXTON / BERRI

Berri Hotel
Riverview Drive, 5343 Berri
📞 08 8582 1411
https://www.berrihotel.com.au
✉ info@berrihotel.com.au
From 77 AU$/night for a twin.

Booky Cliffs Campground
Winkie SA
📞 08 8204 1910
www.parks.sa.gov.au/booking
From 12,50 AU$/night for the campsite.

How to get there?
256 km East of Adelaide
 From 40 AU$ (3h45)
 2h45

NURIOOTPA

BIG4 Barossa Tourist Park
Penrice Rd, Nuriootpa
📞 08 8562 1404
https://barossatouristpark.com.au
From 40 AU$/night for the campsite.

TASMANIA

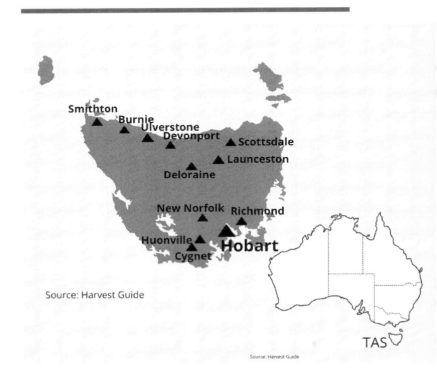

Source: Harvest Guide

TAS

Source: Harvest Guide

Where to go depending on the season?

In Burnie, **high demand between January and June** for vegetables (average demand for the rest of the year), **between December and May** for berries (average demand in November).
Average demand for apples between February and April, for cherries between December and February.

In Deloraine, high demand between December and April for berries (average demand in May), **between January and June** for vegetables (average demand for the rest of the year).

In Devonport, high demand between January and June for vegetables (average demand for the rest of the year).
Average demand for cherries in December and January, for berries between December and April and for apples between March and May.

In Huonville, high demand between March and May for apples, **in December and January** for cherries (average demand in February), **between November and May** for strawberries.
Average demand for grapes in March, April and between June and August.

In Launceston, high demand in March and April for apples (average demand in February and May), **in April, july and August** for grapes (average demand in March and May).

In New Norfolk, high demand between December and February for cherries, **in March and April** for hops (average demand in September and October).
Average demand for grapes in March, April and from June to August.

In Richmond, high demand in December and January for stonefruits (average demand in February, March and April), **from January to June** for vegetables (average demand for the rest of the year), **in December and January** for apples and cherries (average demand in February, March and April).
Average demand from March to July for grapes.

In Scottsdale, high demand in March, April and between September and November for hops **and between January and June** for vegetables (average demand for the rest of the year).

In Smithton, high demand between January and June for vegetables (average demand for the rest of the year).

In Ulverstone, high demand between January and June for vegetables (average demand for the rest of the year) **and between December and May** for berries (average demand in November).

High demand			Average demand								
	Jan.	Feb.	Mar.	April	May	June	July	Aug.	Sept.	Oct.	Nov.	Dec.
Burnie												
Deloraine												
Devonport												
Huonville												
Launceston												
New Norfolk												
Richmond												
Scottsdale												
Smithton												
Ulverstone												

Farm addresses and contacts

CYGNET

Tahune Fields Nursery
(28 km North of Cygnet)
106 Lucaston Rd, Lucaston
📞 03 62 66 44 74
f Tahune-Fields-Orchard-Farm

Smith R & R
(26 km North of Cygnet)
«Lollara» 54 Lucaston Rd, Grove
📞 03 62 66 43 39
www.rrsmith.com.au
Andrew:
✉ andrew@raworganics.net.au

Lucaston Park Orchards
(28 km North of Cygnet)- apples
33 Lucaston Rd, Lucaston TAS
📞 03 62 66 44 12
f lucastonparkorchards
✉ lucastonparkorchards@gmail.com

Groombridge, Peter
(22 km East of Cygnet)
Trial Bay TAS 7155
📞 03 62 67 44 69

Tassie Blue Blueberries
79 Cygnet Coast Rd, Lymington
📞 03 6295 0082
f Tru-Blu Berries

FARM ADDRESSES AND CONTACTS | TASMANIA

Trial Bay Orchards (apples)
26 km East of Cygnet.
3160 Channel Hwy, Kettering TAS
📞 03 62 67 44 69

Glenburn Orchards Pty Ltd
(apples and cherries)
7254 Channel Hwy, Cygnet
📞 03 62 95 04 35
Apply directly on the website
www.glenburnorchards.com.au
✉ admin@glenburnorchards.com.au

Eden Farmstay
22 Supplice Rd, Cygnet
📞 03 6295 0716
www.edenfarmstay.com.au
✉ edenorchard@bigpond.com

Hartzview Vineyard
70 Dillons Rd, Gardners Bay
📞 03 6295 1623
www.hartzview.com.au
✉ enquiries@hartzview.com.au
f Hartzview Vineyard

HUONVILLE

R J & P C Hankin
(33 km South of Huonville)
450 Sledge Hill Rd, Glendevie TAS
📞 04 28 97 63 42

BW Griggs & Sons (apples)
2873 Huon Hwy, Huonville TAS
📞 03 62 64 14 74
✉ office@fruitgrowerstas.com.au
www.fruitgrowerstas.com.au

Calvert Bros (apples)
Ranelagh TAS 7109
📞 03 62 64 22 67

Cane D T & D M
(11 km South of Huonville)
3238 Huon Hwy, Franklin TAS
📞 03 62 66 31 70
f Cane-D-T-D-M

Scott Brothers
(25 km South of Huonville)
322, Scotts Road, Cairns Bay TAS
📞 03 6297 1230
✉ aw.scott@bigpond.com
www.facebook.com/scottbrosfarm

Francis M & F
(40 km South of Huonville)
Francis Town Rd, Dover TAS 7117
📞 03 62 98 15 19

Lucaston Park Orchards
26 Lucaston Rd, Lucaston
📞 03 6266 4412
f Lucaston Park Orchards
✉ lucastonparkorchards@gmail.com

Oaksun Cherries
41 Narrows Rd, Strathblane
☎ 03 6298 1420

3rd Rock Agriculture
799 North Huon Rd, Judbury
☎ 03 6266 6272

Woodstock Cherries Pty Ltd
8624 Channel Hwy, Woodstock
☎ 0408 951 773
www.woodstockcherries.com.au

Home Hill Winery
38 Nairn Rd, Ranelagh
☎ 03 6264 1200
www.homehillwines.com.au
✉ info@homehillwines.com.au

Oaksun Cherries Tasmania Pty Ltd (cherries)
48 km South of Huonville.
41 Narrows Rd, Strathblane TAS
☎ 03 62 98 14 20

Jildon Farm
(25 km South of Huonville)
190 Cygnet Coast Rd, Petcheys Bay
☎ 03 62 95 00 88

Harvest information Service
☎ 1800 062 332
www.harvesttrail.gov.au

LAUNCESTON

Crestview Blueberry Farm
(blueberries)
524 Golconda Rd, Lilydale TAS
☎ 03 63 95 14 07
✉ crestview3@bigpond.com
f Crestview-Blueberries

Legana Orchards Pty Ltd
(13 km North of Launceston)
61 Jetty Rd, Legana TAS 7277
☎ 03 63 30 22 12 or
03 63 30 11 15

Burlington Berries
(40 km South of Launceston)
157 Burlington Rd, Cressy TAS
☎ 03 63 97 65 91
✉ hr@burlingtonberries.com.au
www.burlingtonberries.com.au

Windarra Raspberry Farm
(25 km South of Launceston) -
Strawberries
Cressy Rd, Longford TAS 7301
☎ 04 07 87 74 86
f Windarra-Raspberry-Farm

Aviemore Farm
403 Gravelly Beach Rd, Gravelly Beach
☎ 03 6394 4631

Miller G C & Sons Pty Ltd

(30 km North of Launceston)
291 Main Rd, Hillwood TAS 7252
📞 03 63 94 81 81

Lees Orchard

(apples, pears and berries)
Dilston TAS 7252
📞 036328 1158
✉ office@leesorchard.com.au
𝐟 Lees.Orchard.Dilston

Montague Fresh

38 Jetty Rd, Legana
📞 03 9709 8100
www.montague.com.au/trade-services
✉ support.office@montague.com.au

Top-Qual Calthorpe Orchard

Batman Hwy & Valley Rd, Sidmouth
📞 03 6394 7273

Orchard

15 Spring Hill Rd, Sidmouth
📞 03 6394 7790
✉ michaeljlees@bigpond.com

Leaning Church Vineyard

76 Brooks Rd, Lalla TAS
📞 03 6395 4447
www.leaningchurch.com.au

Brook Eden Vineyard

167 Adams Rd, Lebrina TAS
📞 03 6395 6244
www.brookeden.com.au
✉ mail@brookeden.com.au

Harvest information Service
📞 1800 062 332
www.harvesttrail.gov.au

Pipers Brook Vineyard

1216 Pipers Brook Rd, Pipers Brook
📞 03 6382 7555
www.kreglingerwineestates.com/cellar-door
✉ info@kreglingerwineestates.com

Dalrymple Vineyard

1337 Pipers Brook Rd, Pipers Brook
📞 03 6382 7229
www.dalrymplevineyards.com.au
✉ info@dalrymplevineyards.com.au

Delamere Vineyards

4238 Bridport Rd, Pipers Brook
📞 03 6382 7190
www.delamerevineyards.com.au
✉ info@delamerevineyards.com.au

Tamar Ridge Cellar Door

1A Waldhorn Dr, Rosevears
📞 03 6330 1800
www.tamarridge.com.au/
✉ info@tamarridge.com.au

84

DELORAINE

Christmas Hills Raspberry Farm
(raspberries)-
14 km North of Deloraine.
Bass Hwy, Elizabeth Town TAS
📞 03 6362 2740
✉ info@raspberryfarmcafe.com
Apply directly on the website
www.fruit-pickers-tasmania.com.au
www.raspberryfarmcafe.com
f www.facebook.com/tasberries

DEVONPORT

Sassafras Orchards
(à 20 km au Sud de Devonport)
143 Native Plains Rd, Sassafras
📞 03 64 26 73 73
✉ sassafrasfarms@bigpond.com

Ayers G P & M W Pty Ltd
21 Pilgrims Rd, Spreyton TAS
📞 03 6427 3022

Spreyton Fresh
289 Tarleton Rd, Tarleton
📞 03 6427 2125
www.spreytonfresh.com.au
✉ jobs@spreytonfresh.com.au

Youngs Vegie Shed
317 Bass Hwy, Camdale
📞 03 6431 6087
www.youngsvegieshed.com
f Youngs Vegie Shed - Camdale

Ghost Rock Vineyard
1055 Port Sorell Rd, Northdown
📞 03 6428 4005
www.ghostrock.com.au
✉ sierra@ghostrock.com.au
f Ghost Rock Wines & Cellar Door

Lake Barrington Vineyard
1136 W Kentish Rd, West Kentish
📞 03 6491 1249
www.lakebarringtonestate.com.au
✉ info@lakebarringtonvineyard.com.au
f Lake Barrington Vineyard

SWANSEA

Milton Vineyard
14635 Tasman Hwy, Swansea
📞 03 6257 8298
www.miltonvineyard.com.au
✉ wine@miltonvineyard.com.au
f Milton Vineyard

Spring Vale Vineyard
130 Springvale Rd, Cranbrook
📞 03 6257 8208
www.springvalewines.com
✉ barry@springvalewines.com

HOBART

Granton Berry Farm
(28 km South of Hobart)
23 Eric Crt, Granton TAS 7030
☎ 03 62 75 06 87

Wolfe Bros. Smallfruits
(14 km South of Hobart)
98 Wolfes Rd, Neika TAS 7054
☎ 03 62 39 63 10
f Wolfe-Bros-Smallfruits

Fruit Growers Tasmania
262 Argyle St, Hobart TAS 7000
☎ 03 6169 2059
www.fruitgrowerstas.org.au
Michael Tarbath
✉ admin@fruitgrowerstas.org.au
f FruitGrowersTasmania

Nierinna Blueberries
371 Nierinna Rd, Margate TAS
☎ 03 62 67 25 81
f Nierinna-Blueberries

Wolfes Berry Farm
98 Wolfes Rd, Neika
☎ 03 6239 6310
www.facebook.com/Wolfesberry

Harvest information Service
☎ 1800 062 332
www.harvesttrail.gov.au

Sorell Fruit Farm
(strawberries, apricots, apples, etc)
174 Pawleena Rd, Sorell TAS
☎ 03 6265 3100
✉ sorellfruitfarm@gmail.com
f SorellFruitFarm
www.sorellfruitfarm.com

Pegasus Sprouts
48b Browns Rd, Kingston
☎ 03 6229 7090
www.sproutstas.com.au
✉ pegasus@sproutstas.com.au
f Pegasus-Sprouts

Westerway Raspberry Farm
1488 Gordon River Rd, Westerway
☎ 0447 010 701
www.lanoma.com.au
To apply, fill in the forms on the site
and send them to
✉ WesterwayJobs@hotmail.com

Meadowbank Estate
☎ 0481 147 397
www.meadowbank.com.au
✉ peter@meadowbank.com.au
f Meadowbank - Tasmania

Derwent Estate Vineyard
329 Lyell Hwy, Granton
☎ 03 6263 5802
www.derwentestate.com.au
✉ wine@derwentestate.com.au

Stefano Lubiana Wines
60 Rowbottoms Rd, Granton
📞 03 6263 7457
www.slw.com.au
f Stefano Lubiana Wines & Osteria

RICHMOND

The Ragged Tier Cherry Garden
(cherries)
42 km East of Richmond.
166 Woolleys Rd, Kellevie TAS
📞 03 62 53 51 14

J W Kirkwood Pty Ltd
(8 km North of Richmond)
«Ticehurst» Brown Mountain Rd,
Campania TAS 7026
📞 03 62 60 44 63

Cape Bernier Vineyard
230 Bream Creek Rd, Bream Creek
📞 03 6253 5443
www.capebernier.com.au
✉ info@capebernier.com.au

Frogmore Creek Winery
20 Denholms Rd, Cambridge
📞 03 6274 5844
www.frogmorecreek.com.au
✉ cambridge@frogmorecreek.com.au

Pooley Wines
1431 Richmond Rd, Richmond
📞 03 6260 2895
www.pooleywines.com.au
To apply, please fill in the form
directly on the website.
f Pooley Wines

Craigow Vineyard
528 Richmond Rd, Cambridge
📞 0418 126 027
www.craigow.com.au
✉ info@craigow.com.au
f Craigow Vineyard

BRUNY ISLAND

Bruny Island Berry Farm
(berries)
Adventure Bay Rd, Adventure
Bay
📞 0434 760 325
✉ brunyberries@bigpond.com

Harvest Information Service
📞 1800 062 332
www.harvesttrail.gov.au

Where to stay?

Check if you can stay at the farm

HOBART

The Nook Backpackers
Dormitory: From 25 AUD$/night
251 Liverpool St, Hobart
📞 03 6135 4044
www.thenookbackpackers.com
✉ info@thenookbackpackers.com

Narrara Backpackers Hobart
Dormitory: From 30 AUD$/night
Twin room from 79 AU$/night
88 Goulburn St, Hobart T
📞 03 6234 8801
www.narrarabackpackers.com
✉ info@narrarabackpackers.com

Hobart Central YHA
Dormitory: From 29 AUD$/night
9 Argyle St, Hobart
📞 03 6231 2660
www.yha.com.au
✉ hobartcentral@yha.com.au

Montacute Boutique Bunkhouse
Dormitory: From 47 AUD$/night.
1 Stowell Ave, Battery Point
📞 03 6212 0474
www.montacute.com.au
✉ hello@montacute.com.au

CYGNET / HUONVILLE

Base Camp Tasmania
From 18 AU$/night for the
campsite.
959 Glenfern Rd, Glenfern
📞 03 6261 4971

How to get there?
54 km South of Hobart
🚌 From 11 AU$ (1h08)
🚗 (46 min)

LAUNCESTON

Pod Inn
Single room from 47 AU$/night.
17-19 Wellington St, Launceston
📞 0475 555 549
www.podinn.com.au
✉ booking@podinn.com.au

Launceston Backpackers
Dormitory: From 25 AUD$/night
Twin from 65 AU$/night.
103 Canning St, Launceston
📞 03 6334 2327
www.launcestonbackpackers.com.au
✉ bookings@launcestonbackpackers.com.au

Launceston Holiday Park
711 W Tamar Hwy, Legana
📞 03 6330 1714
www.launcestonholidaypark.com.au
✉ launceston@islandcabins.com.au
From 30 AU$/night for the campsite.

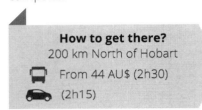

How to get there?
200 km North of Hobart
🚌 From 44 AU$ (2h30)
🚗 (2h15)

DELORAINE

Deloraine Hotel
Emu Bay Road, Deloraine
📞 03 6362 2022
From 47 AU$/night for a single room.
www.delorainehotel.com.au
✉ info@delorainehotel.com.au

Deloraine Apex Caravan Park
51 W Parade, Deloraine
📞 03 6362 2673

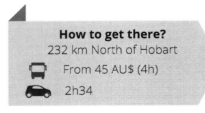

How to get there?
232 km North of Hobart
🚌 From 45 AU$ (4h)
🚗 2h34

DEVONPORT

The Formby Hotel/Alexander Hotels and Backpackers
82 Formby Rd, Devonport
📞 03 6424 1601
Dormitory: From 35 AU$/night.
www.goodstone.com.au/the_formby
✉ formby@goodstone.com.au

Mersey Bluff Caravan Park
41 Bluff Rd, Devonport
📞 03 6424 8655
www.merseybluffcaravanpark.com.au
✉ bookings@mbcp.net.au

How to get there?
282 km North of Hobart
🚌 From 71,60 AU$ (4h45)
🚗 3h06

SWANSEA

Swansea Holiday Park
2 Bridge St, Swansea
📞 03 6257 8148
www.swansea-holiday.com.au
From 35 AU$/night for the campsite.

How to get there?
134 km from Hobart
🚌 From 45 AU$ (2h05)
🚗 1h46

BRUNY

Neck Reserve Camping Area
3003 Bruny Island Main Rd, South
Bruny

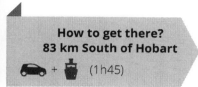

How to get there?
83 km South of Hobart
+ (1h45)

Cloudy Corner campground
South Bruny TAS
0439 106 147

The Pines Campsite
Cloudy Bay Rd, South Bruny

Captain Cook Holiday Park
786 Adventure Bay Rd,
Adventure Bay
03 6293 1128

VICTORIA

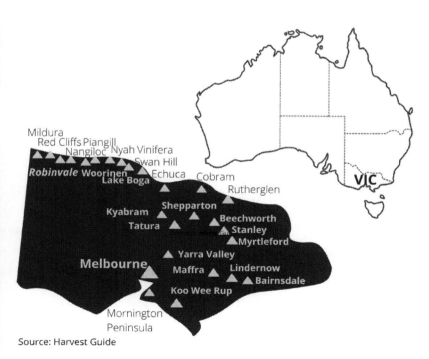

Source: Harvest Guide

Where to go depending on the season?

In Bairnsdale / Lindenow, high demand from October to March for vegetables (average demand for the rest of the year).

In Beechworth, high demand in November and December for cherries. Average demand between March and May for apples, between February and April and between June and August for grapes, in March and April for hazelnuts.

In Cobram, high demand between January and April for apples and pears (average demand in May), **in November and December** for cherries, **between January and April** for stonefruits (average demand in May and December).
Average demand all year round for lemons and vegetables.

In Echuca, hig demand in February and Mars for tomatoes (average demand in January and April).

In Koo Wee Rup, high demand between September and December for asparagus.

In Maffra, average demand between October and April for vegetables.

In Mildura, high demand between June and August for lemons (average demand between September and January and in May), **between February and April and between June and August** for grapes (average demand in May and September), **in October and November** for vegetables (average demand between December and February and between May and September).

In Myrtleford, high demand in March and April for the hops. Average demand for apples between January and April, in March and April for hazelnuts, in February, March and between June and August for grapes.

9

In the Mornington Peninsula, high demand in December and January for cherries (average demand in November), **between November and April** for the raspberries.
Average demand between March and November for apples, between December and March for berries, between February and April for grapes.

In Nangiloc, high demand between June and August and November and December for lemons (average demand in January, May, September and October), **from February to April and June to August** for grapes (average demand in January, May and September), **in October and November** for vegetables (average demand between December and February and between May and September).

In Nyah, high demand between June and August and in November and December for lemons (average demand in January, May, September and October**), between February and April and between June and August** for grapes (average demand in January, May and September), **between December and February** for stonefruit (average demand between May and September and in November).
Average demand for vegetables between May and February.

In Robinvale, high demand between January and April and between June and August for grapes, **in April, May and September** for pistachios and almonds (average demand in March and June).
Average demand for vegetables between May and February.

In Rutherglen, high demand in November and December for cherries. Average demand for apples between March and May. Between February and April, and between June and August for grapes.

In Warragul, average demand all year round for tomatoes, and in February for apples.

In Shepparton, high demand in February and March for stonefrui (average demand in January), **in February and March** for apples and pears (average demand in January, April and May), **in February and March** for tomatoes (average demand in January and April).
Average demand in November and December for cherries, and between January and March for vegetables.

In Swan Hill, high demand in June, July and between October and December (average demand in January, May, August and September), **between February and April and between June and August** for grapes (average demand in January, May and September) **between November and February** for stonefruit (average demand between May and July and in October), **in April and May** for pistachio and almonds (average demand in March and June).
Average demand for vegetables between May and February.

In the Yarra Valley, high demand between February and May fo apples and pears.

High demand			Average demand									
	Jan.	Feb.	Mar.	April	May	June	July	Aug.	Sept.	Oct.	Nov.	Dec.
Bairnsdale / Lindenow												
Beechworth												
Cobram												
Echuca												
Koo Wee Rup												
Maffra												
Mildura												
Mornington Peninsula												
Myrtleford												
Nangiloc												
Nyah												
Robinvale												
Rutherglen												
Shepparton												
Swan Hill												
Warragul												
Yarra Valley												

Farm addresses and contacts

YARRA VALLEY

Yarra Valley Hillbilly Farms
Cnr Parker & Monbulk Silvan
Roads, Silvan VIC 3795
📞 03 97 37 95 39
✉ hillbilly.farms@live.com

Byrnes Hillndale Orchards
(apples)
120 Quayle Rd, Wandin North VIC
📞 03 5964 4549

Cherryhill Orchards (cherries)
474 Queens Road, Wandin
East, Victoria 3139
📞 03 59 64 42 35
✉ jobs@cherryhill.com.au
www.cherryhill.com.au
For picking, contact Mali Hang at
1300 934 866
✉ mali.hang@chandleragribusiness.com.au

Fresco Fresh (raspberries)
35 km East of Yarra Valley.
300 Station Rd, Wesburn VIC 3799
📞 03 5967 2222
www.frescofresh.com.au
✉ frescofresh.info@gmail.com
f frescofreshstrawberries

Chappies (cherries,raspberries, blackberries, etc.)
21 - 23 Parker Rd, Silvan VIC 3795
📞 03 97 37 95 34
✉ enquiries@upick.com.au
www.upick.com.au
f chappiesupick

Blue Hills Berries & Cherries
27 Parker Rd, Silvan
📞 03 9737 9400
http://upickberries.com.au
✉ info@upickberries.com.au
f Blue Hills Berries and Cherries

Seville Hill Orchard
8 Paynes Rd, Seville
📞 03 5964 3284
www.sevillehill.com.au
f Seville Hill Wines
✉ info@sevillehill.com.au

Rieschieck Orchards (apples)
13 Medhurst Rd, Gruyere
📞 03 5964 9369

Maroondah Orchards
715 Maroondah Hwy, Coldstream
📞 03 9739 1041

Berry Plant Suppliers
25 Phillips Rd, Toolangi
📞 03 5962 9316

Jay Berries - U Pick
140 Wandin Creek Rd, Wandin East
📞 03 5964 4451
www.jayberries.com.au
𝐟 Jay Berries
✉ info@jayberries.com.au

Johns Orchards Farm Work
Cambus Rd, Yering
📞 03 9739 1570

Kookaberry Strawberry Farm
25 Lewis Rd, Wandin
📞 0415 768 222
www.kookaberry.com.au
𝐟 Kookaberry Berry Farm

Perry Certified Strawberry Runner Growers
1826 Healesville-Kinglake Rd, Toolangi
📞 03 5962 9429

Brooklyn Orchards Pty Ltd
Apples and pears
525 Tarrango Road, Gladysdale
📞 03 59 66 63 27
✉ jaquijohn@bigpond.com

Napoleone M V & Co Pty Ltd
Lemons, plums, tropical fruits
Rouget Rd, Wandin North
📞 03 59 64 45 96
www.redrichfruits.com.au

Wandin Vale Orchards
Lot 56 Charteris Rd, Wandin East
📞 04 18 38 01 12

S R Shaholli
Apples and pears
New Dookie Rd, Shepparton
📞 03 58 21 26 59

Harvest Information Service
📞 1800 062 332
www.harvesttrail.gov.au

SHEPPARTON

Erinhaven Orchard
Cnr Maneroo & Nathalia Rds, Bunbartha
📞 03 58 26 94 66

D P & H L Stephens
(17 km North of Shepparton)
Nathalia Rd, Bunbartha VIC 3634
📞 03 58 26 95 05

N M & B J Barolli (apples and pears)
165 Hosie Rd, Shepparton East
📞 03 58 29 24 22

Rockington Orchard
(86 km East of Shepparton)
Lot 1 Greta West Rd, Glenrowan
📞 04 57 66 23 51

FARM ADDRESSES AND CONTACTS | VICTORIA

R P & M A Puckey
(apples and pears)
37 km West of Shepparton
«Summerlands»
Palmer Rd, Kyabram VIC 3620
03 58 52 11 62

Farmwell Tomatoes Pty Ltd
Tomatoes
301 Harston Rd, Harston
03 58 54 83 65

Harvest Labour Assistance
MADEC Australia
Suite 1 & 4, 461
Wyndham Street Shepparton
03 5829 3600

Bisogni F (lemons)
Torgannah Rd 3644 Cobram
03 58 72 11 13

Fruitworks (tomatoes)
0358 215 688
Cnr Corio & Stewart Sts,
Shepparton
f www.facebook.com/fruitworksshepparton

Diretto Orchards Pty Ltd
Benalla-tocumwal Rd, Yarroweyah
03 58 73 23 71

Smith & Sons
«Passchendaele» Orchard Warby
Range Rd, Glenrowan VIC 3675
03 57 66 23 35

Rullo Orchards Pty Ltd
470 Old Dookie Rd,
Shepparton East
03 58 29 24 44

Hamilton P H & Son
Ardmona Rd, Ardmona VIC 3629
04 09 93 75 24

Seeka Australia Pty Ltd.
4765 Barmah-Shepparton Rd,
Bunbartha
03 5826 9636

S T & R Varapodi
Cnr Turnbull & Lenne Rds, Ardmona
03 58 29 00 83

Planet Produce
625 Midland Hwy, Shepparton East
03 58 29 22 41

Nashi Haven
McPhersons Rd, Bunbartha VIC
04 58 26 94 36

Besim & Sons (apples & pears)
106 Thompsons La, Kyabram
📞 03 58 52 14 84

J & N Nicosia (apples)
Catona Crs, Cobram VIC
📞 04 58 72 16 83

J V Orchards
383 Campbell Rd, Cobram
📞 03 58 72 22 87
f JV-Orchards

Scenic Drive Strawberries
(strawberries)
Torgannah Rd, Koonoomoo VIC
📞 04 58 71 12 63

H. V McNab & Son
pears, peaches, apples
145 Ardmona Rd, Ardmona
📞 03 58 29 00 16
✉ mail@mcnab.com.au
www.mcnab.com.au
Please apply on the website.

Ardmona Orchards Pty Ltd
325 Cornish Rd, Ardmona
📞 03 58 29 02 83

Pickworth Orchards
282 Ferguson Rd, Tatura
📞 03 58 24 25 32

Boris Fruit Shed (tomatoes)
Benalla Rd, Shepparton East VIC
📞 03 58 29 24 88
f BorisFruitShed

Gibbs K J
Invergordon VIC 3636
📞 03 58 65 53 05

Finer Fruit (tomatoes)
35 Vaughan St, Shepparton VIC 3
📞 03 58 31 13 78
f finerfruitshepparton
✉ inerfruitshepparton@gmail.com

OzPac Australia Pty Ltd
(12 km from Shepparton)
540 Turnbull Rd, Ardmona VIC
📞 03 5820 7600
✉ gregd@ozp.com.au
f Ozpac-Australia-Pty-LTD

Crosbie Orchards
(apples, pears)
300 Macisaac Rd, Ardmona VIC
📞 03 58 29 03 52

Belstack Strawberry Farm
80 Bennetts Rd, Kialla West VIC
📞 03 5823 1324
www.belstackstrawberryfarm.com

Tranquil Hills Orchards (lemons)
70 Wyatt Rd 3644 Cobram East
📞 04 29 17 96 39

ACN Orchards (apples)
Nathalia Rd, Bunbartha VIC
📞 03 58 26 94 37
𝐟 ACN Orchards

Jefsand park Lucerne
55 Ebbott Rd, Shepparton East
📞 0418 551 212
www.jefsand-park-lucerne.business.site

Red River Rural (breeder)
37 McGill St, Shepparton
📞 01300 068 067
www.redriverrural.com.au
✉ admin@redriverrural.com.au

Shepp East Fruit Packers
Lot 662 Midland Hwy, Shepparton East
📞 03 5829 2541

Masalki Pty Ltd (orchard)
255 Verney Rd, Grahamvale
📞 03 5821 1637

ARANA INTERNATIONAL
(wine wholesaler)
13 Banks Pl, Shepparton
📞 0401 501 919

Parris G M & Sons (apples)
New Dookie Rd, Shepparton VIC
📞 03 58 21 2185

Super Fresh Australia
(apples, pears)
610 Channel Road, Shepparton
📞 0424 883 767
✉ superfresh@westnet.com.au
www.super-fresh.com.au

Sunny Ridge Strawberry Farm
244 Shands Rd, Main Ridge VIC
📞 03 59 89 45 00
www.sunnyridge.com.au
✉ info@sunnyridge.com.au

P & A Vigliaturo Orchards
540 Simson Rd, Ardmona
📞 03 58 29 01 63

Murray River Produce
Murray Valley Hwy, Cobram VIC
📞 03 58 72 12 52

Greenwood L M & J E
«Greenwood Orchards» Main Rd,
Merrigum VIC 3618
📞 03 58 55 23 41

D MacHeda
Healy Rd, Yarroweyah VIC 3644
📞 03 58 72 23 75

Plunkett Orchards

(pears, apples, apricots, peaches, nectarines)
255 Mcisaac Rd Ardmona, VIC
📞 03 58 29 00 15
www.plunkettorchards.com.au
Apply directly on the page
www.employment.plunkettorchards.com.au

Poulos Orchards (apples)

Doyles Rd, Shepparton VIC
📞 03 58 31 30 89
f Poulos-Orchards

Kutrolli Z & J (apples)

Mc Phee Rd, Shepparton
📞 03 58 21 23 51

Al Badry (apples)

1 Twisden Ct, Shepparton VIC
📞 03 58 22 07 20

Silverstein M & R (berries)

131 Prentice Rd, Shepparton East
📞 03 58 29 23 07

Boosey Fruit Pty (apples)

Chapel Rd, Cobram VIC 3644
📞 03 58 73 53 90

Gattuso G (apples)

Cobram VIC 3644
📞 03 58 72 11 70

Turnbull Bros Orchards Pty Ltd

Apples, pears, cherries
65 Turnbull Lane, Ardmona
📞 03 58 29 00 02
✉ admin@turnbullbrothers.com.au
www.turnbullbrothers.com.au

SPC Factory Sales

197-205 Corio St, Shepparton
📞 03 5821 7033
www.spcfactorysales.com.au
✉ info@spcafactorysales.com.au

LAKE BOGA/ SWAN HILL/ NYAH

Butler Orchards Pty Ltd

(12 km from Swan Hill)
Athorn Rd, Woorinen VIC 3589
📞 03 50 37 62 38

Harvest Labour Assistance

MADEC Australia
183-188 Beveridge Street
Swan Hill
📞 1800 062 332
✉ swanhill@madec.edu.au

Narrung Orchards

1 Murray Valley Hwy, Narrung VIC
📞 03 50 38 82 52
f Narrung-Orchards

FARM ADDRESSES AND CONTACTS | VICTORIA

W J Barbour
Nyah VIC 3594
📞 03 50 30 25 25

Winter G J
Scown Rd, Tresco West VIC
📞 03 50 37 21 78

Riverbend Orchard
3655 Murray Valley Hwy,
Wood Wood
📞 03 50 30 53 85

Chislett Farms
833 Kenley Rd, Kenley
📞 03 5038 8238
www.chislettfarms.com.au

B P Duffy
67 McAlpines Rd, Nyah VIC
📞 03 50 30 23 67

AROUND MELBOURNE

Bon View Orchards Pty Ltd
Apples and pears
Browns Rd, Officer
📞 03 59 43 23 56

Brimbank Orchards Pty Ltd
(13 km West of Melbourne)
280 Sunshine Rd, Sunshine VIC
📞 03 93 11 81 17
f Brimbank-Orchards

Taranaki Farm
(70 km North of Melbourne)
5 Falloons Rd, Woodend VIC
📞 0409 980 438
www.taranakifarm.com.au
✉ shop@taranakifarm.com.au

Sunny Creek Fruit Berry Farm
(130 km East of Melbourne)
69 Tudor Rd, Trafalgar West VIC
📞 03 56 34 75 26

Tuckerberry Hill (berries)
97 km South of Melbourne
31 Becks Rd, Drysdale VIC 3222
📞 03 52 51 34 68
www.tuckerberry.com.au
f TuckerberryHill
✉ tuckerberry@bigpond.com

Dinny Goonan Wines (grapes)
880 Winchelsea-Deans
Marsh Rd, Winchelsea South
📞 03 5288 7100
www.dinnygoonan.com.au

Statewide Fruit Picking
21 Baynton Crs, Roxburgh Park
📞 04 22 80 39 88
f Statewide Fruit Picking

Hand Picked Fruit & Veggies
181 Reynolds Rd, Doncaster East
📞 03 98 42 31 11

Brimbank Orchards Pty Ltd
280 Sunshine Rd, Sunshine
📞 03 93 11 81 17

The Big Berry
925 Gembrook-Launching Pl Rd,
Hoddles Creek
📞 03 5967 4413
www.thebigberry.com.au
f The Big Berry

Aumann Family Orchard
Apples and pears
246 Tindals Rd, Warrandyte
📞 03 98 44 34 64
✉ contact@aumannsproduce.com.au
www.aumannsproduce.com.au

Warrandyte Berry Farm
(34 km East of Melbourne)-
raspberries, blackberries.
449-451 Ringwood-Warrandyte Rd,
Warrandyte South
📞 0409 411 402
f warrandyteberryfarm
✉ warrandyteberryfarm@gmail.com

Chaplin's Orchard
123 km North of Melbourne
Chaplins Rd, Harcourt
📞 03 54 74 22 64
f Chaplin Orchards

Nippy's Fruit Juices Pty Ltd
Oranges
Essendon North VIC 3041
📞 03 93 38 49 69
www.nippys.com.au

Just Picked Berries & Fruit
80 Old Plenty Rd, Yan Yean
📞 04 12 63 65 35
✉ info@justpicked.net.au
www.justpicked.net.au

ECHUCA

Bolitho L J (apples)
Bolitho Rd, Kyabram VIC 3620
📞 03 58 52 11 37

MILDURA / RED CLIFFS / NANGILOC

B R&C L McGinniskin
Loop Rd, Nichols Point VIC
📞 03 50 23 08 63

J Surace
Cowra Ave, Irymple VIC 3498
📞 04 17 390 613

Lloyd Owen & Janice
Benetook Ave, Mildura VIC
📞 03 50 23 34 67

Cavallo L
Newton Ave, Red Cliffs VIC
03 50 24 21 78

Koola Grove (berries)
Iraak Rd, Nangiloc VIC
03 50 29 16 89

Currans Family Wines (grapes)
10 km from Mildura.
3391 San Mateo Ave, Koorlong
03 50 25 71 54

Mammone V
Belar Ave, Irymple VIC
03 50 24 56 38

F S Thatcher
Red Cliffs VIC 3496
03 50 24 14 12

Harvest Labour Assistance
MADEC Australia
Cnr 10th Street and Deakin
Avenue Mildura
1800 062 332
harvest@madec.edu.au

Dichiera C & M
Blk 504, Red Cliffs
03 50 24 16 34

Westridge Farm
Kulkyne Way, Iraak VIC 3494
03 50 29 15 54

F Radman
Red Cliffs VIC 3496
03 50 24 15 80

P M Dichiera
Calder Hwy, Merbein
03 50 25 26 28

D J & K G McManus
Red Cliffs VIC 3496
03 50 24 12 47

Deakin Estate
1596 Kulkyne Way, Iraak
03 9682 5000
www.deakinestate.com.au
deakin@wingara.com.au

Frank Sos
Colignan VIC 3494
04 27 10 54 40

R P Barich
Merbein South VIC
03 50 25 64 70

Castles Crossing Orchards
(lemons)
Castles Crossing Rd, Nangiloc
03 50 29 14 56

P Brizzi
Azolia St, Red Cliffs VIC 3496
📞 03 50 24 16 66

R J Treen
Birdwoodton VIC 3505
📞 03 50 25 62 12

Panagiotaros A & A
Cowra Ave, Mildura VIC 3500
📞 03 50 23 15 64

Cavallo L
Red Cliffs
📞 03 50 24 21 78

Cavallaro F D & P
Etiwanda Ave, Koorlong VIC
📞 03 50 25 72 58

Strubelj F & D
Benetook Ave, Mildura VIC 3500
📞 04 50 22 21 22

Tall Poppy Wines
140 A Lime Ave, Mildura
📞 03 5023 5218
www.tallpoppywines.com
f Tall Poppy Wines

STANLEY / BEECHWORTH

G A Primerano
1700 River Rd, Whorouly VIC
📞 03 57 27 12 13

Nightingale Bros
(apples and pears)
708 Morses Creek Rd, Wandiligong
📞 03 5750 1595
www.nightingalebros.com.au
✉ admin@nightingalebros.com.au
(season from February to May)

J Christesen
Buckland Rd, Beechworth VIC
📞 03 57 28 17 48

Bright Berry Farms (apples)
40 km South of Stanley
Great Alpine Rd, Eurobin
📞 03 57 56 25 23
f Dessert-Shop/Bright-Berry-Farms

Sinclair Orchards Pty Ltd
(apples)
Beechworth Rd, Stanley VIC
📞 03 57 28 65 01
✉ sinclairapples@bigpond.com

Harvest Information
Service
📞 1800 062 332
www.harvesttrail.gov.au

10

High Grove (apples)
Mt Stanley Rd, Stanley VIC 3747
📞 03 57 28 65 26
www.higrove.com.au
✉ info@higrove.com.au

R J Tully (apples)
30 Tully Rd, Beechworth
📞 03 5728 1392

Rosewhite Kiwifruit Orchard
(apples)
RMB 2785 Rosewhite Rd,
Myrtleford
📞 03 57 53 52 55

Rockington Orchard
(53 km West of Beechworth)
Lot 1 Greta West Rd, Glenrowan
📞 03 57 66 23 51

Blue Ox Blueberries (berries)
77 Smith St, Oxley VIC 3678
📞 03 5727 3397
f Blue-Ox-Berry-Farm

Hilton H
Main Rd, Stanley VIC 3747
📞 03 5728 6584

MAFFRA

Gippsland Greenhouse Produce
(eggplant, tomatoes)
105 km from Maffra.
Highway, Yarragon Victoria 3823
📞 04 27 186 288
✉ info@gippslandgreenhouse.com.au
f Gippsland-Greenhouse-Produce

WARRAGUL

Newman's Berries
(raspberries, blueberries,
blackberries)
21- 27 School Rd, Erica VIC
📞 0400 392 550

ROBINVALE

A Natale
Hocking Rd, Robinvale VIC 3549
📞 03 5026 3978
f Natale-Farms

O'Brien P W & P M
Blk 96c, Robinvale VIC
📞 03 50 26 14 86

Brigante Bros
Robinvale South VIC 3549
📞 03 5026 4080
f Brigante-Bros

Zara C
Lake Powell, Bannerton
☎ 03 50 26 93 50

Olam Orchards Australia
(almonds)
2 Perrin St, Robinvale
☎ 03 50 26 33 44

A H & E J Conner
Murray Valley Hwy, Boundary Bend
☎ 03 50 26 82 24

Zappia R
Newbriatan Rd, Robinvale VIC
☎ 03 50 26 31 29

Harvest Labour Assistance
MADEC Australia
68 -72 Herbert Street
Robinvale
☎ 1800 062 332
✉ robinvale@madec.edu.au

Robinvale Organic Wines
243 Robinvale-Sea Lake Rd,
Robinvale
☎ 03 5026 3955
www.organicwines.com.au
✉ info@organicwines.com.au

Bogicevic Michael (vegetables)
☎ 0350 260 228
Murray Valley Hwy, Wemen

Olivegrove Trading Company
☎ 0350 263 814
Tol Tol Rd, Robinvale VIC
www.robinvaleestate.com.au
✉ oil@robinvaleestate.com.au

MORNINGTON PENINSULA

Drum Drum Blueberry Farm
28 Davos St Main Ridge
☎ 03 59 89 62 08
www.drumdrumfarm.com.au
✉ drumdrumfarm@gmail.com

Mock Red Hill (apples)
1103 Mornington-Flinders Rd,
Red Hill VIC 3937
☎ 03 59 89 22 42
www.mockredhill.com.au
✉ enquiries@mockredhill.com.au

Berrydale Farm (grapes)
21 km from the Mornington
Peninsula.
125 Victoria Rd, Pearcedale VIC
☎ 03 59 78 62 16
f Berrydale-Farm

Flinders Farm (tomatoes)
2071 Boneo Rd Flinders VIC
☎ 03 59 89 00 47
✉ ffarm@cdi.com.au

Atlanta Fruit Sales Pty Ltd

(apples)
1194 Stumpy Gully Road
Moorooduc
📞 03 59 78 83 74
✉ atlanta@surf.net.au
www.yvfruits.com.au

Staples R & A

(apples and pears)
144 Roberts Rd, Main Ridge
📞 03 59 89 62 55
www.staplesapples.com.au
✉ staples@staplesapples.com.au

Tamarillo Fruit Farm

100 Barcus Rd,
Main Ridge VIC 3928
📞 03 95 92 80 75

Red Hill Cherry Farm

69 Prossors Ln, Red Hill
📞 03 5989 2237
www.redhill-cherryfarm.com.au
f trevorholmes@pac.com.au

LAHARUM

Grampians Olive Co. (Toscana)

376 Olive Plantation Road
LAHARUM
📞 03 53 83 82 99
✉ info@grampiansoliveco.com.au
www.grampiansoliveco.com.au

BAIRNSDALE

FruitFarm Johnsonville

(apples, cherries, nectarines,
peaches, pears, plums)
17 km East of Bairnsdale.
54 Bumberrah Rd, Johnsonville
📞 03 5156 4549

BALLARAT

Buninyong Blueberry Farm

7189 Midland Hwy, Buninyong
📞 04 09 31 67 24
✉ ernie@buninyongblueberries.com.au
www.buninyongblueberries.com.au
f Buninyong Blueberry Farm

Glenlyon Nutty Fruit Farm

18 Spring St, Glenlyon
📞 03 53 48 75 42

BENDIGO

McLean Bros Glencoe Orchards
Apples and pears
Danns Rd, Harcourt VIC
📞 03 54 74 26 58

> Harvest Information
> Service
> 📞 1800 062 332
> www.harvesttrail.gov.au

KOO WEE RUP

Santo & Maria Giardina
3 Bickerton La, Mirboo North
📞 03 56 64 83 52

SMOKO

Gunnadoo Berries
Smoko Via, Bright VIC 3741
📞 03 57 59 25 07
f Gunnadoo Berries

Where to stay? **Check if the farm can accommodate you**

MELBOURNE

United Backpackers Melbourne
250 Flinders St, Melbourne
📞 03 9654 2616
www.unitedbackpackers.com.au
Dormitory: From 38 AUD$/night

Melbourne Central YHA
562 Flinders St, Melbourne
📞 03 9621 2523
www.yha.com.au
✉ melbcentral@yha.com.au
Dormitory: From 36 AUD$/night

Flinders Backpackers
35 Elizabeth St, Melbourne
📞 03 9620 5100
www.flindersbackpackers.com.au
✉ info@flindersbp.com.au
Dormitory: From 26 AUD$/night
Twin room from 80 AU$/night

Space Hotel
380 Russell St, Melbourne
📞 03 9662 3888
www.spacehotel.com.au
✉ stay@spacehotel.com.au
Dormitory from 38 AUD$/night

107

Habitat HQ
333 St Kilda Rd, St Kilda
 03 9537 3777
www.habitathq.com.au
Dormitory: From 32 AUD$/night.

YARRA VALLEY

Enclave at Healesville Holiday Park
322 Don Rd, Badger Creek
03 5962 4398
From 38 AUD$/night for the campsite.
www.enclavelifestylevillage.com.au
✉ info@enclavelv.com.au

BIG4 Yarra Valley Park Lane Holiday Park
419 Don Rd, Healesville
03 5962 4328
www.parklaneholidayparks.com.au
From 60 AU$/night for the campsite.

How to get there?
64 km East of Melbourne
 From 9 AU$ (3h)
 1h

It is recommended to have your own transportation in the Shepparton area and the Yarra Valley.

Victoria Lake Holiday Park
536 Wyndham St, Shepparton
03 5821 5431
From 28 AUD$/night for the campsite.
www.viclakeholidaypark.com.au
✉ info@viclakeholidaypark.com.au

Strayleaves Caravan Park
Cnr Old Dookie Road and, Mitchell St, Shepparton
03 5821 1232
www.strayleavescaravanpark.com.au
✉ info@strayleavescaravanpark.com.au
From 34 AU$/night for the campsite for a van, 20 AU$/person for a tent.

BIG4 Shepparton Park Lane Holiday Park
7835 Goulburn Valley Hwy, Kialla
03 5823 1576
www.parklaneholidayparks.com.au
From 43 AU$/night for the campsite.

To find the nearest campsite, download the application
WIKICAMPS
www.wikicamps.com.au

Moira Park Camp Ground
7 Moira Dr, Kialla West VIC

How to get there?
190 km North of Melbourne
From 23 AU$ (2h35)
2h

MILDURA

Apex RiverBeach Holiday Park
435 Cureton Ave, Mildura
03 5023 6879
From 33 AUD$/night for the campsite.
www.apexriverbeach.com.au
holiday@apexriverbeach.com.au

BIG4 Golden River Holiday Park
199/205 Flora Ave, Mildura
03 5021 2299
www.goldenriverholidaypark.com.au
From 39 AU$/night for the campsite.

BIG4 Mildura Getaway - Holiday Park Mildura
478 Deakin Ave, Mildura
03 5023 0486
www.big4.com.au/caravan-parks
From 39 AU$/night for the campsite.

Waterview Caravan Park
199 Ranfurly Way, Mildura
0427 955 886

The Palms Caravan Park
7 Cureton Ave, Mildura
03 5023 1774
www.thepalmscaravanpark.com.au
palmscp@bigpond.net.au
From 26 AU$/night for the campsite.

Calder Tourist Park
775 Fifteenth St, Mildura
03 5023 1310
www.caldercp.com.au
bookings@caldercp.com.au
From 32,50 AU$/night for the campsite.

How to get there?
542 km North of Melbourne
From 66 AU$ (8h30)
5h46

MORNINGTON PENINSULA

Capel Sound Foreshore
Point Nepean Road, Foreshore Office, Capel Sound
03 5986 4382
www.capelsoundforeshore.com.au
From 29 AU$/night for the campsite.

Whitecliffs To Camerons Bight
Rye VIC 3941
📞 03 5985 3288
www.whitecliffs.com.au
✉ admin@whitecliffs.com.au

Balnarring Beach Foreshore
154 Balnarring Beach Rd,
Balnarring Beach
📞 03 5983 5582
www.balnarring.net
✉ balnarringforeshore@bigpond.com
From 35 AU$/night for the
campsite.

Point Leo Foreshore Camping
Point Leo Rd, Point Leo
📞 03 5989 8333
www.pointleo.com/camping-information-2
✉ info@pointleo.com

How to get there?
76 km South of Melbourne
🚌 From 22 AU$ (2h50)
🚗 1h

ROBINVALE

Robinvale Riverside Caravan Park
25 McLennan Dr, Robinvale
📞 03 5026 4646
www.robinvaleaccommodation.com.au
✉ info@robinvaleriverside.com.au
From 25 AU$/night for the campsite.

Riverfront Caravan Park
27 Murray Terrace, Euston
📞 03 5026 1543

How to get there?
468 km North of Melbourne
🚌 From 56 AU$ (7h30)
🚗 5h30

BAIRNSDALE

Lake King Waterfront Caravan Park
67 Bay Rd, Eagle Point
📞 03 5156 6387
www.lakekingwaterfront.com.au
✉ lkwcaravanpark@gmail.com
From 30 AU$/night for the
campsite.

Nicholson River Holiday Park
915 Princes Hwy, Nicholson
📞 03 5156 8348
www.nicholsonriver.com.au
✉ info@nicholsonriver.com.au
From 34 AU$/night for the
campsite.

How to get there?
283 km East of Melbourne
🚌 From 30 AU$ (3h50)
🚗 3h12

WESTERN AUSTRALIA

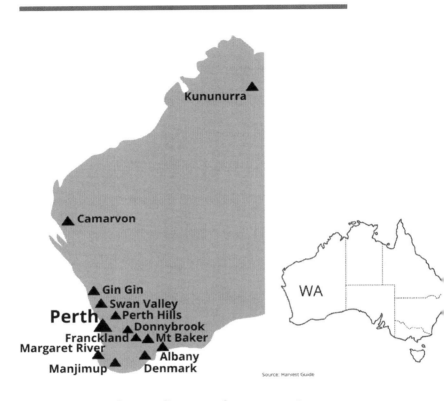

Source: Harvest Guide

Where to go depending on the season?

In Albany, high demand from November to February for strawberries (average demand between March and May and in October).
Average demand between May and August for olives, in April and May and between June and September for grapes.

In Busselton, high demand in September and October for avocados (average demand in August, November and December).
Average demand between May and January for potatoes. Between February and April, then between June and August for grapes. 111

In Carnarvon, high demand between May and December for tomatoes, **between January and March** for melons (average demand in April), **in January and February** for mangoes (average demand in March, May and October), **in June and July, then between October and December** for grapes and vegetables (average demand in May, August and September).
Average year-round demand for bananas.

In Denmark, average demand for berries between December and March, for grapes between February and April, then between June and September.

In Donnybrook, high demand between December and March for stonefruit (average demand in November).
Average demand for apples and pears all year round except January and October, for grapes between February and April and June and September, for tomatoes between February and April.

In Frankland, high demand in July and August for grapes (average demand between February and April, in June and September). Average demand between May and August for olives.

In Gingin, average demand all year round for lemons and vegetables, in January and February, and between June and August for grapes. Between July and September for olives. Between November and January for the stonefruit.

In Kununurra, strong demand for mangoes in October and November (average demand in December), **between July and October** for melons/pumkin (average demand in May, June and November). Average demand in April for lemons, between April and July for tree plantations.

In Manjimup, high demand in March and April for apples and pears (average demand in February and May), **in December** for stonefruit (average demand in January and February), **between December and March** for vegetables.
Average demand for potatoes between October and June, for avocados between December and February.

In Margaret River, high demand between February and April for the harvest (average demand between June and August).

In Moora, high demand in October and November for lemons.
Average demand from November to February for stonefruit.

In Mount Barker, strong demand between November and February for strawberries (average demand between March and May, and in October), **in July and August** for grapes (average demand in March, April, June and September).
Average demand between November and January for cherries.

In Perth Hills, average demand between November and April, and between June and August for apples and pears.
Average demand between October and March for stonefruit.

In the Swan Valley, strong demand between July and August for the harvest (average demand in January, February, June and September).
Average demand all year round for lemons and vegetables, for olives between July and September, and for stonefruit in November and December.

High demand			Average demand									
	Jan.	Feb.	Mar.	April	May	June	July	Aug.	Sept.	Oct.	Nov.	Dec.
Albany												
Busselton												
Carnarvon												
Denmark												
Donnybrook												
Frankland												
Gingin												
Kununurra												
Manjimup												
Margaret River												
Moora												
Mount Barker												
Perth Hills												
Swan Valley												

Farm addresses and contacts

AROUND PERTH

Farm Fresh
(salads, cucumbers)
U4/ 27 Jacquard Way, Port Kennedy
08 95 24 55 08
sales@hcfarmfresh.com.au
www.hcfarmfresh.com.au

Stoneville Blueberry Farm
(Stonefruits)
240 Blue Wren Pl, Stoneville
08 92 95 07 67

Avowest Avocados
85 Carabooda Rd, Carabooda
08 94 07 51 00

Citrees Nursery (lemons)
12B Lakefarm Ret, Ballajura
08 92 48 60 03

Della-Pona E
Mundaring Weir Rd, Kalamunda
08 92 93 13 27

Berry Sweet Strawberry Farm
(strawberries)
Bullsbrook WA 6084
08 95 71 10 77
f Berry-Sweet-Strawberry-Farm
admin@berrysweet.com.au

Illawarra Orchard Pty Ltd
(apples, pears)
233 Illawarra Rd, Karragullen
08 93 97 60 94

114

Agrifresh Pty Ltd
(lemons, stonefruits)
Unit 12/ 41 Catalano Cct,
Canning Vale
☎ 08 94 55 45 38
www.agrifresh.com.au
✉ job@agrifresh.com.au

Canning Orchard Pty Ltd
Brookton Hwy Cnr Gardiner Rd,
Karragullen
☎ 08 93 97 59 19

Leotta Nominees Pty Ltd
(Leotta's Fresh Stone Fruit)
741 Canning Rd, Carmel WA
☎ 0408 904 950
f www.facebook.com/Leottas
✉ leotnom@bigpond.com

Gullone D
Union Rd, Carmel WA 6076
☎ 08 92 93 52 18

Hills Market Garden Nominees
Lot 6 Canning Mills Rd, Kelmscott
☎ 08 93 90 57 54

Yanchep Springs (blackberries)
Lot 2818 Wanneroo Rd,
Wilbinga WA 6041
☎ 08 95 75 76 65

C W & J E Brockway
Llanelly Organic
Orchard Brockway Rd, Roleystone
☎ 08 93 97 56 33

Golden Grove Citrus Orchad
1378 Chittering Road
Lower Chittering 6084
☎ 08 95 71 80 74
✉ info@goldengroveorchard.com
www.goldengroveorchard.com.au

Kato's 3000 Grapes
3000 W Swan Rd, Caversham WA
☎ 0431 596 489
f Kato's at 3000

Choice Strawberrys
Shed, Carabooda WA 6033
☎ 08 95 61 8335

Edgecombe Bros Ltd (grapes)
Lot 1715 Gnangara Rd, Ellenbrook
☎ 08 92 96 43 07
✉ info@edgecombebrothers.com.au
www.edgecombebrothers.com.au

Fawcett Orchards (lemons)
Scarp Rd, Serpentine WA 6125
☎ 08 95 25 23 15
f Fawcett-Orchards

Harvest Information
Service
☎ 1800 062 332
www.harvesttrail.gov.au

115

High Vale Orchard Pty Ltd
(apples)
35 Merrivale Rd, Pickering Brook
📞 08 92 93 82 17
✉ bookings@corecider.com
www.highvale.com

Willow Springs Orchard Pty
408, Albany Hwy, Bedfordale WA
📞 08 93 99 51 15
www.wso-orchard.com.au
✉ tony123wso@gmail.com
f Willow Springs Orchard Farm

Raeburn Orchards
Nectarines, peaches, cherries...
95 Raeburn Rd, Roleystone
📞 08 93 97 53 25
www.raeburnorchards.com
✉ enquiries@raeburnorchards.com
f Raeburn Orchards

Gregorovich D & N
Patterson Rd, Pickering Brook
📞 0892 93 83 01

KUNUNURRA

Ceres Farm
512 Packsaddle Rd, Kununurra
📞 08 9168 1613
www.ceresfarm.com.au

Harvest Labour Assistance
📞 08 9168 1500

Parker Poynt Plantation
(mangoes)
479 Jabiru Rd, Kununurra
📞 0891 691 388

Cummings Brothers
📞 0891 681 400
Research Station Rd, Kununurra

Bluey's Outback Farm
📞 0891 682 177
✉ blueysoutbackfarm@bigpond.com
www.blueysoutbackfarm.com.au

Bardena Farms
📞 0409 691 505
384 Packsaddle Rd KUNUNURRA

Barradale Farm
📞 0891 691 386
✉ barradale@wn.com.au

BUSSELTON/ DONNYBROOK

Glendalough Orchards
(Apples)
📞 0897 311 273
38 Irishtown Rd, Donnybrook

Fruit Barn (Tomatoes)
📞 0897 311 198
7 South Western Hwy, Donnybrook
f www.facebook.com/Fruitbarn
✉ sales@thefruitbarn.com.au

116

Anstey Orchards
Goodwood Rd, Capel WA
📞 08 97 31 71 01
f Anstey Orchards

Karintha Orchards Pty Ltd
(apples, pears)
South West Hwy, Kirup WA
📞 08 97 31 01 06
✉ karinthaorchards@bigpond.com
www.karinthaorchards.com.au

Harvey Citrus Pty Ltd (lemons)
RMB 4026 Fifth St, Harvey WA
📞 08 97 29 38 61
www.harveycitrus.com.au
✉ harveycitrus@icloud.com

Hazel Grove Orchard
(apples)
RMB 317 Tweed Rd, Bridgetown
📞 08 97 61 19 21
f Hazel Grove Orchard

Atherton's Orchard Pty Ltd
(apples, pears)
Preston Rd, Lowden WA
📞 08 97 32 12 37

Martella B & Sons
«Santa Rita», Kirup WA
📞 08 97 31 62 76

Tassone Orchards Pty Ltd
Grimwade Rd, Kirup WA 6251
📞 04 28 97 50 21

Hawter Bros
Hawterville Rd, Mullalyup
📞 08 97 64 10 69
f Hawter Bros

Sunvalley Orchards
(apples, pears)
RMB 629, Donnybrook WA
📞 08 97 31 11 74

Terace G & Sons (apples)
South Western Hwy, Donnybrook
📞 08 97 31 1159

Jones LA
709 Charlies Creek Rd, Donnybrook
📞 08 97 31 15 12

Barton Jones Wines
39 Upper Capel Rd, Donnybrook
📞 0409 831 926
www.bartonjoneswines.com.au
✉ info@bartonjoneswines.com.au

Perivale Orchards Pty Ltd
The Upper Capel Rd, Donnybrook
📞 08 97 31 63 21
f Perivale Farm

Delfino G
RMB 624 Boyupbrook Rd,
Donnybrook
08 97 31 11 69

Swanto Orchard
0897 311 021
297 South Western Hwy,
Donnybrook

SWAN VALLEY

**Stoneville Blueberry
Farm** (Stonefruit)
0892 950 767
240 Blue Wren Pl, Stoneville

**Grape Growers
Association Of W.A.** (grapes)
0892 964 993
PO Box 179, Herne Hill WA

Kafarela's
706-712 Great Northern Hwy,
Herne Hill
08 9296 0970

Sittella
100 Barrett St, Herne Hill WA
08 9296 2600
www.sittella.com.au
info@sittella.com.au

Windy Creek Estate
27 Stock Rd, Herne Hill WA
08 9296 1057
www.windycreekestate.com.au

Jarrah Ridge Wines
651 Great Northern Hwy, Herne Hill
08 9296 6337
www.jarrahridge.com

Talijancich Wines
26 Hyem Rd, Herne Hill WA
08 9296 4289
www.taliwine.com.au
admin@taliwine.com.au

Valley Wines
352 Lennard St, Herne Hill WA
08 9296 1147
www.valleywines.net.au

Olive Tech International (Olives)
0417 984 470
PO Box 3098, Broadway WA

MARGARET RIVER

Xanadu Wines
316 Boodjidup Rd, Margaret River
08 9758 9500
www.xanaduwines.com

Redgate Wines

659 Boodjidup Rd, Margaret
River WA
☏ 08 9757 6488
www.redgatewines.com.au
✉ info@redgatewines.com.au

Voyager Estate

41 Stevens Rd, Margaret River
☏ 08 9757 6354
www.voyagerestate.com.au
✉ wineroom@voyagerestate.com.au

CARNARVON

Sweeter Bananas

1945 N W Coastal Hwy, North
Plantations WA
☏ 08 9941 9100
www.sweeterbanana.com

Gascoyne Gold Pty Ltd

424 N River Rd, North
Plantations WA
☏ 08 9941 8209
f Gascoyne Gold Pty Ltd

Bumbak & Son

☏ 0899 418 006
f Bumbak & Sons

Harvest Information Service
☏ 1800 062 332
www.harvesttrail.gov.au

ALBANY

Montgomery's Hill Wines

☏ 08 9844 3715
Hassell Hwy, Kalgan WA
www.montgomeryshill.com.au
✉ winesales@montgomeryshill.com.au

Bunn Vineyard & Winery

☏ 08 9842 6266
www.bunnwine.com.au
✉ admin@bunnwine.com.au

Wignall's Wines

☏ 0898 412 848
448 Chester Pass Rd, Albany
www.wignallswines.com.au
✉ info@wignallswines.com.au

Genovese Olive Co

☏ 0418 932 824
Chesterpass Rd, Albany WA

Eden Gate Blueberry Farm

(blueberries)
Eden Rd, Youngs Siding WA
☏ 08 98 45 20 03
✉ info@edengate.com.au
www.edengate.com.au

ATC Work Smart
5 Barker Road Albany WA
☏ 08 6819 5300
www.atcworksmart.com.au

Willow Creek Strawberries Pty Ltd (strawberries)
984 Dempster Rd, Albany WA
📞 08 98 46 43 00
✉ job@agrifresh.com.au
www.agrifresh.com.au/home

Handasyde N M (strawberries)
Lot 2 Greatrex St, Lower King
📞 08 98 44 34 19
✉ neil@handasydestrawberries.com.au
www.handasydestrawberries.com.au

DWELLINGUP
(100 km South of Perth)

Oro Farms (apples, pears)
Oro Rd, Dwellingup WA
📞 08 95 38 10 15

Giumelli Steven
Polybrook Rd, Dwellingup WA
📞 08 95 38 10 67

Where to stay?

Check if the farm can host you !

PERTH

Ocean Beach Backpackers
1 Eric St, Cottesloe WA
📞 08 9384 5111
www.oceanbeachbackpackers.com.au
✉ backpackers@obh.com.au
Dormitory from 24 AU$/night.
Twin room from 81 AU$/night.

Hostel G Perth
80 Stirling St, Perth WA
📞 0402 067 099
www.hostelgperth.com
✉ reservations@hostelgperth.com
Dormitory from 29 AU$/night.

Koalas Perth City Backpackers Hostel
286 Hay Street East Perth
📞 0417 260 398
www.koalasperth.com
Dormitory from 17 AU$/night.
Twin room from 47 AU$/night.

Spinners Hostel
342 Newcastle St, Perth
📞 08 9328 9468
www.spinnershostel.com.au
✉ admin@spinnershostel.com.au
Dormitory from 28 AU$/night.

The Emperors Crown Hostel
85 Stirling St, Perth WA
📞 08 9227 1400
www.emperorscrown.com.au
✉ manager@emperorscrown.com.au
Dormitory from 18 AU$/night.
Twin room from 62 AU$/night.

The Witch's Hat
148 Palmerston St, Perth
📞 08 9228 4228
www.witchs-hat.com
✉ manager@witchs-hat.com
Dormitory from 26 AU$/night.

Haus Accommodation
42 Francis Street, Northbridge
📞 08 9228 8170
Dormitory from 23 AU$/night.
Family room (3 persons) from 59 AU$/night.

The Shiralee
107 Brisbane Street, 6003 Perth
📞 08 9227 7448
Dormitory from 22 AU$/night.
Twin room from 58 AU$/night.

Perth City YHA
300 Wellington St, Perth
📞 08 9287 3333
www.yha.com.au
✉ perthcity@yha.com.au
Dormitory from 27 AU$/night.

KUNUNURRA

Kona Lakeside Caravan Park
Lakeview Dr, Kununurra

Discovery Parks - Lake Kununurra
Lakeview Dr, Kununurra WA
📞 08 9168 1031
www.discoveryholidayparks.com.au

Hidden Valley Caravan Park
110 Weaber Plain Rd, Kununurr
📞 08 9168 1790
www.hiddenvalleytouristpark.com
✉ nhvtp@westnet.com.au
Prices on request.

How to get there?
✈ From 269 AU$
(3h10 from Perth)
🚗 10h from Darwin

BUSSELTON / DONNYBROOK

Dunsborough Beachouse YHA
201-205 Geographe Bay Road, 6281 Dunsborough
📞 08 9755 3107
Dormitory from 38 AU$/night.

Dunsborough Inn Backpackers

50 Dunn Bay Road, 6281
Dunsborough
📞 08 9756 7277
www.dunsboroughinn.com.au
✉ bookings@dunsboroughinn.com.au
Quadruple room from
37 AU$/night.

How to get there?
223 km South of Perth
🚌 From 63 AU$ (3h45)
🚗 2h18

SWAN VALLEY

Swan Valley Rest Cottage29

Toodyay Rd, Middle Swan
www.swan-valley-rest cottage.business.site
From 72 AU$/night the three-
bedroom apartment.

Discovery Parks - Lake Kununurra

Lakeview Dr, Kununurra WA
📞 08 9168 1031
www.discoveryholidayparks.com.au

Discovery Parks - Swan Valley

91 Benara Rd, Caversham
📞 08 9279 6700
www.discoveryholidayparks.com.au
From 32 AU$/night the campsite.

How to get there?
14 km North East of Perth
🚌 From 9 AU$ (45 min)
🚗 22 min

MARGARET RIVER

Margaret River Backpackers YHA

66 Townview Terrace, 6285
📞 08 9757 9572
Margaret River Town
Dormitory from 32 AU$/night.

Margaret River Tourist Park

44 Station Rd, Margaret River
📞 08 9757 2180
www.summerstar.com.au
✉ info@margaretrivertouristpark.com.au
Reservation and prices by email.

RAC Margaret River Nature Park

Bramley National Park, Carters Rd,
Margaret River
📞 08 9758 8227
www.parksandresorts.rac.com.au
From 50 AU$/night the campsite.

How to get there?
270 km South of Perth
🚌 From 77 AU$ (4h30)
🚗 3h

To book your bus ticket, go to :
www.southwestcoachlines.com.au
www.integritycoachlines.com.au

CARNARVON

Coral Coast Tourist Park
108 Robinson St, Carnarvon
08 9941 1438
www.coralcoasttouristpark.com.au
info@coralcoastpark.com
From 39 AU$/night for the
campsite.

Carnarvon Caravan Park
477 Robinson St, Carnarvon
08 9941 8101
www.carnarvonpark.com.au
bookings@carnarvonpark.com.au

Outback Oasis Caravan Park
49 Wise St, Carnarvon
08 9941 1439
www.outbackoasis-caravanpark.com
outbackoasis@westnet.com.au
From 25 AU$/night for the
campsite.

How to get there?
900 km South of Perth
 From 170 AU$ (12h30)
9h40

ALBANY

Acclaim Albany Holiday Park
550 Albany Hwy, Albany
08 9841 7800

Albany Gardens Holiday Resort
22 Wellington St, Albany
08 9841 4616
www.albanygardens.com.au
info@albanygardens.com.au
From 53 AU$/night for the
campsite.

BIG4 Emu Beach Holiday Park
8 Medcalf Parade, Albany
08 9844 1147
www.big4emubeach.com.au
From 32 AU$/night for the
campsite.

How to get there?
415 km South of Perth
4h45

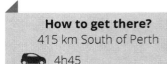

To find the nearest campsite,
download the application
WIKICAMPS
www.wikicamps.com.au

Printed in Great Britain
by Amazon